The Welsh Illusion

for Menna

The Welsh Illusion

Patrick Hannan

seren

seren
is the book imprint of
Poetry Wales Press Ltd
Wyndham Street, Bridgend, Wales

ISBN 1-85411-205-8

A CIP record for this title is available from
the British Library

*The publisher works with the financial assistance of the
Arts Council of Wales*

Cover design by Simon Hicks

Printed in Plantin by WBC Book Manufacturers, Bridgend

Seren gratefully acknowledges the assistance of BBC Wales
in producing this book

Contents

Acknowledgements

This book is based on a series of radio documentaries broadcast in the autumn of 1996 and I'm particularly grateful to the then Editor of Radio Wales, Nick Evans, for commissioning it and for making it possible for me to find the time to do the necessary work. Owen Smith worked with me for some months as the producer, and didn't give up even when, on two separate occasions and in two separate pubs in Aberaman, he drank the worst pints of bitter he had ever tasted. He worked long into the night to get the first programmes made until he was rescued by translation to the *Today* programme in London. Alistair McGhee was then generous enough to take on the rest of the series. At that time and since I've had good reason to be grateful for his reassuring skills, both technical and editorial. Liz Colayera somehow found the time to transcribe the interviews and always turned out to have done so before I thought it was possible. I risked almost thirty years of friendship by asking Trevor and Penny Fishlock to read the text, which they did with a characteristic combination of openness, sympathy and thoroughness.

My wife, Menna, was both tactful and firm in the face of considerable provocation, particularly when presented with sections of manuscript at times when she had more pressing matters to attend to. Her contribution to this book and all that lies behind it cannot be overstated. Many people freely gave their time to be interviewed by me in the course of the radio series. I cannot thank them enough, especially those who have also allowed me to quote them in this book. They are acknowledged in the text to which they give substance.

Introduction

In his unauthorised biography of Michael Heseltine, Julian Critchley includes the surprising information that Heseltine "... can do a good imitation of a Swansea docker". Quite what qualifications Critchley has to judge this rare talent are not clear, but it's a striking declaration all the same because it's one of the few moments in which Heseltine's Welshness gets a look-in during an account of a career which took him tantalisingly close to the top of the political tree. It's true that Heseltine has made it clear that he's proud of having served in the Welsh Guards, although his enthusiasm for soldiering didn't even extend to his finishing his two years' national service. Part of the way through it he chose instead to fight the Gower constituency in the 1959 general election, a decision which meant he had to leave the army prematurely.

Which suggests that, in his own view and that of many others, Heseltine is perhaps not really Welsh but willing to help out when they're busy. That is no doubt why, on February 23, 1996, as Deputy Prime Minister and a member of the Millennium Commission, he felt he could risk a quick trip to his native country. Nothing travels faster than a politician with good news in his pocket. So he turned up in Cardiff for a few hours to reveal that the commission had allocated forty-six million pounds towards the one hundred and six million pounds needed to rebuild the National Stadium (better known as Cardiff Arms Park), the international rugby ground in the centre of Cardiff. No doubt in his long exile Heseltine had come to the same view as Lloyd George who many years before had accused the people of South Wales of suffering from morbid footballism.

William Hague, who at that time was the Welsh Secretary, was apparently of the same mind. The previous October he was reported to have told party workers in Blackpool that he wanted to make Wales a great sporting nation again. Mr Hague was just passing through, so it's unlikely that, even backed by all the resources of the Welsh Office, he would have been able to discover when Wales had last been a great sporting nation. Still, Mr Hague is a politician and therefore entitled to talk rubbish, and is even expected to from time to time.

Not long before Heseltine's visit, on December 22, 1995 Mrs Virginia Bottomley, then the Secretary of State for National Heritage, had announced at a press conference in London that the Millennium Commissioners had decided that among the projects with which the year 2000 would not be marked was the building of an opera house in Cardiff. As a minister Mrs Bottomley was never particularly noted for her sureness of touch, but she might for once have been right when later she turned to a journalist and said: "That'll go down well in Wales." Not with everyone, of course: Lord Crickhowell, the Chairman of the Cardiff Bay Opera House Trust, who as Nicholas Edwards had sat dry-eyed for eight successive years in Mrs Thatcher's Cabinet, is said to have wept tears of rage and frustration at the news. But the average man in Westgate Street hardly blinked as he turned the pages of the *South Wales Echo*.

These two events were supposed to have been unconnected, but even the dimmest boy in the class would have recognised that Cardiff was never going to be awarded two large slices of the Millennium cake and that in these circumstances the populist choice would win. Why build something in which Lord Crickhowell and his establishment chums could watch fat people singing in Italian when you could instead offer the common people a kind of sporting temple in which, amid the most lavish facilities imaginable, they could watch Welsh teams being humiliated year after year?

The important thing about this strange competition doesn't lie in whether the right choice was made, because there's no definitive answer to that kind of question of judgement, but in what it told us about Wales and the kind of society we live in or imagine we live in. And furthermore, the kind of society other people imagine we live in.

For example, those who wanted an opera house believed that one of the reasons their bid failed was because of that very title. It did seem elitist. It did stir up questions of class which are not dead but only sleeping. It didn't take much imagination to visualise the lines of black cars disgorging cargoes of toffs in evening dress for a heavily subsidised evening in Zaha Hadid's challenging building. "The only thing she's ever built is a German fire station", opponents would state derisively. What was puffed as "the crystal necklace" turned out to be a crystal noose.

Later, the opera house supporters realised that they'd got their public relations strategy badly wrong. If only they'd called it a lyric theatre instead of an opera house, they said, then perhaps unwary taxpayers wouldn't have been quite so sniffy about it. That seems to me not only to imply a rather low view of the level of public intelligence but a lack of confidence in the whole scheme. Why shouldn't people be persuaded, for example, that an opera house is something that would add to the dignity of their own lives, even if they never went there?

There was a time when people might have been proud to have an opera house built in their name – after all there's even one amid the breezy vulgarity of Blackpool, in which I've seen the TUC and Ken Dodd on the same day – and cherished it as a badge of enterprise and taste. It would certainly chime with the traditional Welsh view of themselves as poor people with a firm grasp of social and cultural values which transcends their economic and educational circumstances. It is the case, too, that until Cool Cymru produced the flowering of rock bands which shouted about their Welshness, opera productions were among the few Welsh events of any kind you could find taken seriously in the English newspapers. And while people like to bathe in the reflected glory of Bryn Terfel and the many other Welsh singers with international reputations, they don't like to think too much about how they get there in the first place.

There are different kinds of misunderstandings about Welsh rugby which has for years excelled in propaganda rather than achievement. It has created an alternative reality, a paranormal version of rugby and its administration, in which that extraordinary organisation, the Welsh Rugby Union, has contributed so much to low comedy by its consistent ability to see life through the wrong end of a telescope. For a long time, for example, the WRU insisted that it was running an amateur game, a statement which tested the credulity of anyone capable of reading anything more testing than *Janet and John*. Then it invented methods of payment called 'packages' and 'trust funds' so that players might receive money but at one and the same time remain amateurs. This was, we were assured, entirely consistent with the rules of the (amateur) Welsh Rugby Union. After a while this system broke under the stress (perhaps of keeping a straight face) and the game was declared professional. The only problem was there was nothing like enough money available to pay players the kind of wages to which they thought they were entitled. Bankruptcy loomed (and in some cases occurred) but somehow the WRU continued to go round with its hands in its pockets and whistling, like a delinquent school-boy feigning innocence.

All this was bad enough, but it was also an illustration of the way in which people have failed to understand the significance of rugby in Welsh folklore. Big stadiums and professional players in sponsored cars have no place in it. The important point once was that rugby represented a small nation's defiance, its cheek, in the face of opponents who had superior natural supplies of everything but spirit. This is why, for example, people in Wales find themselves unsympathetic to the big, strong, thumping outside half, however appropriate he might be to the modern game and however many points he might score. They want the romance of a slight figure ghosting his way past the desperate clutches of astonished opponents who feel he would break in their hands if only they could get hold of him. That's as much wishful thinking as reality, perhaps, but it represents the way in which Wales has believed it can assert its identity in a wider society which would otherwise swamp it.

That's one version of the myth, anyway, and we have to remember that Welsh rugby is a game in which losing against some opponents can be presented as a form of winning. (See Wales v South Africa, November 1998.) But it seems to me that opera and rugby, placed in that particular false competition and embroiled in the wrong arguments, represented any number of misapprehensions about the character of Wales and its people, misapprehensions which colour the views of people both inside and outside the country itself. There is a distaste for dispersing the shimmering reflection of romance with the stone of argument.

For example, I've heard politicians extrapolate a national char-acter from the tiny fact that there is in Welsh the expression *chwarae teg*, fair play. It thus demonstrates, they say, that there is a sense of social justice in Wales that does not have its counterpart in, say, England (where, as it happens, they have the expression *play the game*). From this argument it's only a short journey to the invention of the natural egalitarianism of Wales which explains the country's general adherence to socialism. This is just another version of Mam and male voice choirs and it flies in the face of everything we know. Labour, yes. Socialism, no. Some of our politicians are as egotistical, vain, lascivious and corrupt as anyone else's. Others are just as selfless, open-minded, hard-working and scrupulous people as you'll discover anywhere.

Then again, it's a matter of received wisdom that there is a conspiracy, masterminded in England, to deprive a wider world of the products of Welsh creative genius, particularly when it comes to writers who discover that London publishers find their products strangely resistible. Any criticism – of plotting, character, dialogue or prose style for example – is simply a metropolitan code for 'too Welsh'. One of the problems about this is that it's difficult to discover exactly who these talented but neglected writers are. In any case, even if it has some truth, writers' problems are chiefly a reflection of the pathetic state of publishing of all kinds in Wales, where surely the impetus should begin, rather than of that in England.

It is in such things and others there is a mythology of Wales, often sentimentally cherished, that can provoke cries of resentment and outrage when it is questioned. But the inescapable fact is that there has never been a more important time for asking questions than now. It's all the more difficult to get a grip on Welsh life because of the way the tide has rushed in over the last couple of decades and demolished so many familiar landmarks. Most of us no longer live in the society we grew up in. Paradoxically, the past is being taken away from us just as we are beginning to discover it.

Many of the certainties have been erased. The industries which once defined Wales have largely disappeared, along with much of the evidence that they ever existed at all. That process has brought with it social change which has eroded community and people's sense of place. Religion is virtually meaningless for most people under fifty. They don't even have a chapel or a church in the background *not* to go to. Class divisions have been altered by changes to education and attitudes, although they have not been destroyed.

The last two decades in particular have altered the roles of, and the relationships between, men and women. They've meant unprecedented affluence for some but at the same time even grimmer poverty and isolation for others. Where the characteristic disease of deprivation of large parts of industrial Wales was once tuberculosis, it's now heroin.

Welsh politics remains recognisable and utterly different at one and the same time because there is now a specific Welsh agenda and a specific Welsh institution in which to shape it. It's difficult to overstate the way in which a Welsh assembly is likely to change our ideas about our lives and how they are run. Partly it is because the assembly will provide a Welsh focus that has never existed before, Welsh affairs run by people solely answerable to Welsh voters. The assembly won't decide everything, of course; it won't decide levels of taxation, for example, but it will pervade our lives soon enough. It won't be long, because that's how politics works, before it begins to test its own limits. And even before that what will its judgements be, for example, on language or the arts? How might it weigh up the competing claims of, say, opera and rugby? Many people might not like the answers because more democracy doesn't necessarily mean an easier life.

The creation of the assembly is the most significant change in a process during which Wales seems, looking back, to have altered at breakneck speed and to have done so, not simply in the creation of new institutions, but in the way in which people have increasingly come to confront the Welsh dimension of public life. That was startlingly underlined by what followed the encounter on Clapham Common on October 26, 1998, between Ron Davies, then the Secretary of State for Wales, and a passing Rastafarian. What exactly happened on that night had them chopping down Amazon rainforests to provide enough paper on which to print the lurid speculation that pursued him, but facts were rather harder to come by. Even the most sympathetic observers (and there were many) found it difficult to see why someone who had done nothing morally or legally wrong but who had, through "a lapse of judgement", found himself in the position of being robbed at knifepoint, should have felt obliged to resign from the Cabinet and why, indeed, the Prime Minister should have accepted that resignation without demur. Nor, later, could the same observer understand why, if nothing had happened, the childhood beatings administered to Davies by his father should somehow be to blame. To blame for what?

These are the sort of deep waters in which expensive lawyers feed, and after a short time the words "Clapham Common" ceased to draw an instant cackle of recognition from current affairs quiz show audiences. The Ron Davies affair was soon enough pushed up into the attic with the debris of all the other half-remembered political scandals of the 1990s. Nevertheless it had consequences which unexpectedly revealed the extent to which Wales had changed and the direction it was now taking.

Throughout that summer Ron Davies had fought an exhausting campaign for the Labour leadership in the assembly against Rhodri Morgan, the MP for Cardiff West, a man whose independence of mind and inability to refrain from saying what he thought was explanation enough for his unexpected exclusion from office in 1997, despite years of dedicated work as an Opposition spokesman. His arresting use of language can't have helped either. Asked by Jeremy Paxman on the *Newsnight* programme if he was standing for Labour leadership in Wales, Morgan answered: "Does a one-legged duck swim in circles?" Paxman looked puzzled. "Is that Welsh for yes?"

The Ron 'n' Rhodri contest was traditional enough, carried on throughout the summer to the point of exhaustion, with plenty of bad feeling behind the scenes – Welsh Labour politics as everyone had always understood it. What was to follow Davies's abrupt departure from the scene revealed the nature of the new dispensation and the central argument we were all going to have to get used to: where did power now lie?

Alun Michael, the Home Office Minister of State and close associate of Tony Blair who became Welsh Secretary on the afternoon of Davies's resignation, after a short interval revealed that he was now a candidate to lead Labour into the assembly elections. With that announcement came a doctrine no-one had heard before: the incumbent Secretary of State should take over as Labour leader because that would ensure a smooth transition of power from old Welsh Office to new assembly. Later Blair was to come to Wales, declare that Michael was "a great guy" (the very highest form of praise in Blairspeak), and explain that the assembly leadership was a succession post to that of Secretary of State; in effect, there was only one qualified candidate. He did not actually carry a banner saying "Vote for Michael", but he might as well have, despite the disclaimers that it was entirely up to the members of the Labour Party in Wales to elect whoever they liked. Unaccountably, in this atmosphere of hands-off fairness, he did not say that Rhodri Morgan was also "a great guy".

All the while Don Touhig, the secretary of the Welsh Labour group of MPs and a central figure in the organisation of a new selection procedure, told the world over and over again that whatever the method chosen for the new contest, and whoever won, the outcome would have "Made in Wales" written on it. Did he have to say it so frequently, people asked, because there was disbelief in the air? Within the Labour Party and, perhaps more significantly, outside it, people were already engaged in the opening rounds of a new kind of challenge match between London and Cardiff.

Absorbing though the contest itself was, the really important point about these events and those that were to follow is that they provided in microcosm a preview of the kind of arguments that are increasingly going to preoccupy Wales under a changed form of government, however limited that change might be. Should Downing Street intervene (even if it says it's not doing so) in internal Welsh affairs? Should Labour in Wales have greater independence from its parent UK party in conducting its own affairs? That leads you almost immediately to the question of how you resolve conflicts between the aspirations of a Welsh assembly and the authority of a UK government. Should the Welsh Office be expected to follow its normal practice of looking over its shoulder at English ministries and following their lead? Or should it instead strike out on its own? Or again, what should the relationship be between Wales and British institutions? How, for example, should the increasingly centralised broadcasting organisations respond to the need for the democratic reinforcement of a new system and how might the new politics intervene?

Even before a single vote was cast in assembly elections, the consequences for the Labour Party in Wales of what happened on Clapham Common blindingly illuminated the nature of the arguments and issues with which people in Wales would have to begin to grapple. They are both fascinating and demanding.

As such events have unfolded it's often been difficult to separate the important from the inconsequential. We are often too ready for the simple explanation or the familiar one. We don't necessarily see how one event sometimes follows inexorably from another. As Kierkegaard put it: "Life must be lived forwards but can only be understood backwards." For more than thirty years as a journalist of one kind or another I have watched these things happen and described them as best I could. Now, in this book, I think it's time to try and make sense of some of them.

The Posh Part
of Aberaman

The first time I ever went into the British Legion club in Aberaman was on a Saturday afternoon in October 1996. I got a few stranger-in-town funny looks as you might expect, but nothing much more until a woman called across from a nearby table.

"Hey, what was your name on the telly?"

"Patrick Hannan."

"That's right," she said, in the tone of surprised congratulation used by Jeremy Paxman on *University Challenge* when some student has accidentally stumbled on the right answer. In fact congratulations were more properly owed to the woman for her feat of memory, since it was by then many years since I'd made more than a fleeting appearance on the telly. But she'd started something.

"Well, I'll go to hell," one man said.

"Dr Hannan's son," another supplied.

"Oh, I remember Dr Hannan."

"Patrick Hannan."

A little later an elderly man beckoned me across. "How old are you now?" he asked. He looked ancient enough to tell me he'd been a pal of my grandfather, who died in 1908.

"Fifty-five."

"That's right. Same as me."

If this is what's involved in visiting the past, I thought, I want to go home.

Yes, Dr Hannan's son, even at fifty-five, which is a form of identification that in one sense tells you almost as much as you need to know about Aberaman and dozens of places like it. Wherever I went in the time I spent there that autumn, people recalled my father and my mother and my brother, not in a spirit of polite inquiry, but instead slipping into the easy familiarity of shared knowledge. It was rather like casual conversation that had been temporarily interrupted because it was someone's turn to go to the bar.

But all the people we talked of were long dead. My father, for crying out loud, had died nearly half a century previously. Yet when I went to one house a woman disappeared for a moment and returned carrying a signed photograph of him. I hadn't lived in this place for forty-five years and had scarcely visited it for more than twenty, but to return was to feel as though I'd just stepped outside for a moment.

Later I thought that life in Aberaman was perhaps reminiscent of those visits we made to the cinema long ago. We would set off at whatever time we were ready, and therefore often arrive in the middle of the main feature. We'd sit through to the end of it, the advertisements, the news, the B movie, even – in *The Rex* in Aberdare – through the man playing the organ that rose mysteriously from the floor, before eventually seeing the first part of the big picture. Then we'd say: "This is where I came in," and push our way back out into the daylight.

It's a phrase that keeps coming back to you if you go to Aberaman because it's changed so little in the last half century or so: except, that is, in the crucial sense that it no longer has any particular reason for existing at all. Of course there are discernible differences. There's no colliery any more, no crunch of hob-nailed boots on the pavement as the miners walk home in their pit dirt. I can't express how evocative that sound was, how much I would have given to have studs in my shoes, making sparks on the pavement, and how deaf my parents were to any such idea. The tip, known for some reason as Nicky Nacky, has gone, swept away in the guilty rush of derelict land clearances that followed the Aberfan disaster a few miles away in the next valley. Some streets are now gap-toothed, others have houses boarded up, but at the same time they are occasionally jostled by the neat suburban modernity that's made Barratt and Wimpey literally household names throughout the country.

I realise I haven't said where Aberaman is, but in many ways that doesn't matter. It's just another pause for breath on the long road that winds through almost unbroken rows of houses from Pontypridd to the Brecon Beacons. Nowadays you don't even have to see Aberaman as you make that journey. A new road where the railway once ran sweeps you quickly and safely past.

I went to see my brother's friend, Windsor Williams. Born the year after the abdication of Edward VIII, he was inevitably known as Duke; not all Welsh nicknames are as inventive as they're made out to be in legend. But hang on, what on earth was he doing here at all? He shouldn't be in Aberaman. The story is supposed to run like this: the miner's son goes to the grammar school and so breaks away from the grim existence of manual labour underground entering instead a sunlit world of clean hands, dark suits, semi-detached houses, lawn mowers and small British motor cars. We're in classic territory here, *South Wales – The Movie* if you like, even down to Duke's father and the traditional lecture.

"Father's be all and end all was to get some security. Every father told his son not to go down the mine because they didn't want us to go through what they had. My football friends who went to secondary modern school, there was no other option for them. If you didn't have a grammar school education it was the pit or the railway or the army. They didn't have an option. The grammar school boy did. He could work his way up in those days. With a socialist government, he could work his way to the top."

What actually happened we shall find out shortly, but that socialist government was meant to be the key to a new life for Windsor Williams and everyone who lived in Aberaman and, for that matter, everyone who lived in the hundreds of places like it up and down the length of Britain.

"We'll make Winston Churchill smoke a Woodbine every day, when the red revolution comes..." we used to sing, even as very small boys, even those of us who were supposed to be nice middle-class children with parents who voted Conservative. And, as the great war leader was swept from office, people might have been forgiven for thinking that the red revolution had indeed finally arrived.

If 1945 and a Labour majority of 146 didn't in fact turn out to be the date of the arrival of the socialist millennium, at least it looked like a promising start. Fascism had been defeated, bunting had been found who-knows-where to welcome soldiers home, long tables had been dragged out of hiding so that we could mark the defeat of Germany and then Japan with street teas. If that wasn't enough, we were, too, at the beginning of the end of empire.

And in places like Aberaman above all, it looked as though – at long last – workers by hand or by brain would be securing the full fruits of their industry, as Clause Four of the Labour Party constitution then had it. Or more of them than they had secured up to that time, anyway. During a convulsion of nationalisation Labour MPs sang *Cwm Rhondda* as they filed through the voting lobbies in the House of Commons to take the coal industry out of the hands of the owners. As they did so, the owners themselves might well have been singing in their baths at the prospect of generous compensation for what they could already see was a future of diminishing profits.

In the end it didn't seem to be much of a swap, the exchange of private companies like Powell Duffryn – still reviled by people even to this day, its initials said to stand for poverty and death – for people like Lieutenant-General Sir Alfred Godwin-Austen, the first director of the South Western division of the National Coal Board. Powell Duffryn had been one of the private companies that dominated the Aberdare valley in particular and, through a process of amalgamation, had by 1935 become the largest producer of coal in Britain. People began to ask soon enough where they could find the significant difference between the days of the great coal owners like Lord Rhondda, Lord Merthyr and David Davies of Llandinam, and the new state capitalism. On January 1, 1947, they put up notices on the collieries saying they were now managed on behalf of the people, but if you looked into the Chairman's office at the National Coal Board, the man you'd find behind the desk was Lord Hyndley of Leeds who, for fifteen years previously, had been managing director of Powell Duffryn.

People like Arthur Horner, the Merthyr-born, Communist General Secretary of the National Union of Mineworkers, understood clearly what was really going on. In his autobiography, *Incorrigible Rebel*, he wrote: "... we had to realise that the Labour Government, while it did its best to make the nationalisation of the mines a success, had no plan for Socialism. They were out to humanize Capitalism, not to change the system."

Pictures of smiling colliers walking into the sunshine appeared on hoardings, promising a great future in mining, but the new life must have been largely indistinguishable from the past as men – still more than 100,000 of them in South Wales in 1947 – answered the call of the pit hooter and its invitation to hard manual labour as well as the certainty for many of injury and disease.

In these circumstances it's hardly surprising that Windsor Williams's father, and thousands like him, had a burning desire to keep his son out of the pit. And perhaps out of Aberaman, too, because life on the surface held many terrors, real and imagined, of which I was perhaps particularly aware because my father was a doctor, an occupation which in those days was largely unprotected by the modern amenities of tigerish receptionists and the camaraderie of group practice. In those days the doctor and his patients often shared the same streets, living side by side.

The virtual end of the coal industry in South Wales is one of the things that marks the dislocation of the last fifty years or so. It is the most readily understood difference between then and now, but perhaps less so than the way in which so much disease has been relegated almost to folk memory. In the streets our everyday conversations as children were full of the language of illness with which we frightened ourselves and each other, a potent mixture of half-understood fact and superstition.

Everyone knew, for example, that if you cut yourself in the web between thumb and forefinger you'd get lockjaw, from which there was no release but a prolonged and agonising death. But the reality could be just as startling: diphtheria, polio and, above all, tuberculosis, the classic disease of poverty and deprivation. Death was on the doorstep in a way that is unimaginable now, even in many of the poorest areas of Britain, a time when it is possible to grow into late middle age without understanding through experience the nature of bereavement, your own or other people's.

As it turned out the the health service was, with the National Insurance system, really the only monument that identifiably survived from that 1945 Labour government. By the time of the next Labour landslide, in 1997, virtually every nationalised industry had disappeared – closed or privatised or a bit of both.

The National Health Service stands out, though, as one of the instruments – as *the* instrument – that transformed the physical condition of millions of people throughout working-class Britain, and so in many ways the whole nature of their lives, not least in how long those lives lasted. At that time bad health and early death for many people was one of the things that defined areas as working class.

Along with the discovery and refinement of new drugs there were determined programmes of public health improvement – new sewage systems, school meals, school milk, new housing. Aneurin Bevan may be forever associated with the creation of the National Health Service but he held another job simultaneously: as Housing Minister between 1945 and 1950 he was responsible for the building of 800,000 new council houses in Britain. In such ways people's lives were changed in a manner that the wholesale nationalisation of industry and commerce never once threatened to bring about and that science could not have achieved alone.

At this point I was going to turn to the books of statistics and define the nature of this change in terms of things like the decline in the incidence of various diseases and the rate of infant mortality. A moment's reflection suggested that there was little to be gained from rehearsing in detail what is well known and generally accepted. Apart, perhaps, from one tiny example I stumbled across recently, something which illustrates vividly the length of that journey from then to now. Parents of children with whooping cough, a common illness at the time, could in those days take them down to the Aberaman gas works where, with the full co-operation of the management, the wheezing infants were taken inside and allowed to breathe the sulphur fumes which, it was widely believed, would relieve their distress.

Nor was that the only caring contribution made by the company. It also installed a box, complete with gas pipe, in which local people could discreetly and painlessly dispose of unwanted animals. In recent years what have become known as the privatised utilities have lectured us daily with hand-wringing sincerity on their dedication to the every need of their customers, but somehow I can't see the mighty gas companies today doing anything quite as useful for the community as easing the regrettable but necessary passing of Rover or Tiddles.

It's also from such tiny details that we piece together the jigsaw which eventually builds into the simplistic version of life in the South Wales valleys. It not only represents what people who have never been there have come to believe, but to some extent is an image which suits those who know better, real life being such an infuriating and intractable condition. It's the picture most powerfully presented, I suppose, by Richard Llewellyn in *How Green Was My Valley* or A.J. Cronin in *The Citadel* and, most tellingly of all, in the cinema versions of those books which, in both senses of the phrase, deal only in black and white. It isn't wrong but at the same time it isn't right either, and it absolutely refuses to go away. The trouble with clichés is that they reveal the truth and conceal it at one and the same time, and many people prefer not to be troubled too much with the loose ends of reality.

In 1963 I went for a job interview at the TUC in London. I was taken in to see the Assistant General Secretary, Vic Feather – Victor Grayson Hardie Feather, in fact, someone whose name alone was virtually a tour through twentieth-century Labour history. It was one of those days when it was clear from the outset that there was a chasm between me and the stout man from Bradford. Feather was nice enough, although, as I was to discover later in my career when he'd become General Secretary of the TUC and I was an industrial correspondent, he was someone whose moods often occupied that tricky ground between the explosive and the totally impossible.

Among other errors of presentation, I arrived at Congress House in London wearing entirely the wrong kind of suit – Prince of Wales check, I think, with pockets cut at a slant and, I blush to reveal it even after all this time, a flap on the breast pocket. What did I think I looked like? The only excuse I can give is that I was then working for the Council of Industrial Design (later the Design Council) and this was the outfit considered most appropriate for that arty-farty institution by the chaps in the gentlemen's outfitting department of Howells of Cardiff who had sold it to me and put it on my mother's account.

Opposite, Feather had on one of those very dark grey, almost black, suits that most people in his world seemed to wear at that time. We have to remember that this was a little while before Clive Jenkins became the first trade union leader in history to wear a suit which was shiny because it was expensive, rather than because it was old. On Feather's trousers there was a light sprinkling of cigarette ash.

The TUC was one of the many subjects about which I knew hardly anything and so my answers tended to be rather shorter than his questions. Eventually, though, he glanced at what would now be called my CV. His eyes lit up. He'd spotted the bit about South Wales.

"Eeeh," he breathed with an entirely new warmth, "was your dad a miner?"

"Um, no... no." Why did I feel so guilty?

Somewhat crestfallen, he picked his way through a bit more of my life. It emerged that my father had died when I was nine. This cheered him up all over again.

"I suppose," he said, tone of voice and body language urging me to agree with him, "I suppose your mum had a struggle putting you through college?"

"Ah... well... um... well... not really."

Of course I didn't get the job but, I've always wondered, if I had lied, if I'd accepted those clichés being offered me on a plate – and who was to know that my father hadn't laboured underground or that my mother didn't scrub doorsteps to pay for my Latin textbooks? – if I'd told Vic Feather what he so clearly wanted to hear, might I even now be carrying files through the corridors of Congress House wearing my very dark grey, almost black, suit?

Vic Feather was one of many who fell for the wholly erroneous idea that all these places, all these Aberamans, were in effect one and the same place, a series of interchangeable villages peeping out from between the tips through a persistent light drizzle. The truth is rather less convenient, because this is a territory characterised above all by rampant tribalism. Which valley? which town? which village? which street? what number? are the defining questions of the traditional interrogation which establishes how much you dislike or suspect someone who might have been born a matter of a mile or two from you.

People from Aberdare, for example, are known throughout South Wales as snakes, a last abusive vestige, I seem to recall, of a betrayal in some industrial dispute long ago. I was going to say long-forgotten dispute, but around here you can bet that someone will remember in minute detail what it was all about.

Someone once said to my brother: "The trouble with you, Hannan, is that you come from the posh part of Aberaman." If you'd ever been there you'd know that such an idea was pretty preposterous – but not entirely so. Even now I find myself drawn into arguments when someone suggests that the Phurnacite plant, that filthy, sulphurous, coal briquette factory which blighted the landscape all around, was in Aberaman. "It's in Abercwmboi," I would insist crossly in the days before it was closed, although no-one could tell you where one place ends and the other begins and in neither of which I had lived for getting on for forty years. The fact is that you can spit from Aberaman into Abercwmboi. As for Mountain Ash, a couple of miles further down the road, that's just bandit country.

The Labour politician Kim Howells says his mother warned him that people in Mountain Ash said "actually" all the time. "Actually, I'm from Mountain Ash." In places like this a single word can not only mark someone out as alien, but also imply assumptions of superiority, a bad move in an area in which I have never heard anyone suggest that his village, his street even, and the people in it could possibly be in any way inferior to any other place in the known world. As it happens, Kim Howells is from Penywaun, perhaps four miles north of Aberaman, and so himself a distinctly exotic form of life – to me, anyway.

But in Aberaman in those days you didn't have to worry very much about what people were like in Penywaun or Mountain Ash or anywhere else. Although the Red and White bus company's drivers risked their own lives and everyone else's as they tore up and down the valleys, there wasn't the same compulsive sense of movement as there is now. Nor was there much opportunity to indulge it, and in summer you could play cricket in Glamorgan Street, at the back of our house, all day without being interrupted more than once or twice to make way for an intrusive car or lorry.

We all of us understood our places in this village and the

place of this village in the world. A one-horse town, a one-industry community, doesn't spend a lot of time coping with an identity crisis. This was somewhere created by coal mining which in its turn defined the lives of everyone here, not just colliers but teachers, shopkeepers, cinema owners, solicitors, bank managers, doctors and publicans. And despite the nature of the industry on which it was built, an industry in which the fate of the workers was entirely in the hands of the owners, private or public, it is the kind of community that has a persistent appeal, even now as it runs through our fingers.

Indeed, the further we get from it the more its romance grows as teams of restorers are brought in to airbrush out of the picture disturbing matters like the injury, illness and premature death which punctuated the lives of people who, if they couldn't be defined exactly as poor, were of pretty modest means. A coating of sentimentalised yuk has been spread over industrial South Wales, just as cameramen put a smear of Vaseline on the lens to blur the harsh outlines of real life.

Some of its one-time attractions are obvious enough when you look back. In particular the freedom provided by a closed society of this kind, the obverse of its claustrophobia. As small children we could wander all day, unmolested, unthreatened, even after dark as we lurked in the street like comic book urchins with our two penn'orth bags of chips.

Doris Mason, now Doris Williams, and today in her eighties, recalled the kind of incident that could perhaps have happened almost anywhere in the working-class Britain of her childhood.

"As a child I'd play in the river and one day I fell in up to my neck. Somebody hauled me out and they took me home. In those days of course there was always a tub of hot water and they took my dress off and they sat me in front of a big fire with a blanket on while my dress was washed and ironed. Then they put it back on and sent me home so my mother wouldn't know I'd nearly drowned."

Yes, I know we're only two tenors short of a particularly glutinous version of *We'll Keep a Welcome*, but this really was a place in which you could live your life, if you so chose, practically without reference to the outside world. It was true that people could leave their front doors open all day and not be robbed.

And in Lewis Street, a short walk away for most people, you could buy all of life's necessities and then some on top.

"There was a big outfitter's next door – Powells," Doris Williams told me, "and my mother used to have a hat from Paris for Easter. Not only my mother, but other people as well."

A look of disbelief must have crossed my face because she insisted: "They were *genuinely* hats from Paris. We went to church to show the hats off and we would say to my father – 'Are you going to church today?' He'd say, 'No, I haven't got a new hat.' He never went anywhere."

The importance of such reminiscences is that getting a genuine Paris hat, going to church rather than chapel, being in trade rather than manual work, were all part of the subtle relationships and gradations of class that defined your place in society and the attitude of other people towards you. It raises the matter of the posh part of Aberaman and where you might find it: in particular, the teasing question of who were the *crachach*?

That word standing alone, one of the few Welsh words that has survived in the vocabularies of the great majority of Welsh people, is both untranslatable and indispensable if you want to understand both the nature of South Wales society fifty years ago (and perhaps even now, come to that, as applied by newspapers to people like William Hague's father-in-law) and the signposts which helped people understand the way in which they lived. The meaning of *crachach* is paradoxically both clear and elusive. People who know the word know what you mean when you use it, but even extensive use of Welsh language dictionaries doesn't produce a satisfactory definition which captures its full flavour. It means, essentially, the posh; but the self-styled posh, the people who give themselves airs and whose prosperity is almost certainly undeserved, probably achieved at someone else's expense. But even better, it's a word that *sounds* contemptuous, very like spitting.

Were we *crachach*? Up to a point, I suppose. Well, perhaps more than a point. I have a picture at home in which, at the age of about two, and looking a bit truculent I have to say, I am standing with a little girl, the daughter of another doctor who lived a short distance away. Behind us, hands protectively on our shoulders, are two maids in their crisp white aprons. They both lived in our house for most of the week and walked the mile or so home on their half days off. You'd have to be practically royalty today to employ people on that scale. The other child, by the way, was to come to public notice half a century later. Her name was Anne Bullen and for a few days in early 1998 newspapers filled page after page with the story how she had been sacked by the Foreign Secretary, Robin Cook, from her job as diary secretary in an effort to find a suitable job for his mistress. It was, understandably, her turn to look truculent.

But this wasn't some big house, like the colliery manager's just down the road, hidden at the end of a tree-lined drive and called Oaklands, the sort of house name that appeared in Enid Blyton books. It was part of the long terrace that made up Cardiff Road, of which we were number 245. Other people came and went in the house, cleaning, washing clothes by hand, doing the garden, minding the children. In the afternoons, my mother would often play bridge with her friends who would occasionally have their fortunes read in the tea leaves by the strange woman who lived somewhere in the attics of the house next door.

Seen from this perspective it seems almost decadent now, but this is how the middle classes lived their lives in working-class areas in those days. And did so, in some cases, in the heart of an entirely different world from their own. My father's surgery was in Glamorgan Street, one of the places we roamed freely through the day. I didn't know then, in fact I didn't know until Doris Williams told me long afterwards, how other people in Aberaman saw it.

"Glamorgan Street was full of people as poor as church mice. They all got drunk on a Saturday and they'd all fight and squabble but they'd all be the best of friends on Sunday. The fighting and squabbling on a Saturday was part of their entertainment.

"I had a customer and she wanted to take some shoes and she said she lived in Glamorgan Street. Good God, I thought, you don't live in Glamorgan Street – because she looked as though she belonged to the Queen. She'd bought the house without knowing.

"Now this person made her house a nice house, for all it was in Glamorgan Street, and she remained a proper lady, although when she gave me her address I couldn't believe that was where she was from."

Where you lived was just one of the social signals to be analysed. A cousin of my mother's, a headmistress, would mock the pretensions of those (other relatives, of course) who thought tea consisted of cucumber sandwiches – *with the crusts cut off.*

But then again, we wouldn't be *crachach* because we were Catholics, something that remains a deeply suspect condition in many parts of Wales to this day. It somehow made us alien and my father was, after all, Irish. But at the same time we were neither as foreign nor as Catholic as the Italian café owners of South Wales, many of whom maintained their separateness through generations. When, much later, I made a documentary film about them, I was amazed to find that you could step off a valleys street into what was effectively an Italian house with marble floors and the rest of it.

While they were selling the rest of us that great South Wales delicacy, the steamed pie, a challenging mixture of grey mince and soggy pastry, often accompanied by a glass of hot Vimto, a mysteriously spiced fruit drink that was supposed to give you *vim*, see, they were probably eating undreamt of varieties of pasta, spiced sausages, meat without brown gravy and real wine which some of them made themselves. It was many years before we found out that spaghetti didn't necessarily come covered in a vivid sauce in a tin.

The way in which people could pick at questions of status was reminiscent of Aneurin Bevan's famous search for power which turned out to have just left a place as he arrived or never to have been there at all. One aunt thought, for example, that the Williamses who owned the Cambrian lamp factory in Aberdare were undoubtedly *crachach*. That was about as high as our imagination could reach, but there were people of whose existence we were entirely unaware who more properly represented the length of the evolutionary chain of class.

I didn't become aware of it until the mid-sixties when I went out to that golden triangle around Abergavenny where people whose wealth had been piled up in industrial South Wales lived in deeply upholstered comfort and seclusion as they made do on the money that governments had given them for their family coal mines and steelworks.

I went to interview Colonel (later Sir) William Crawshay, wartime spymaster and descendant of one of the greatest of the Merthyr ironmasters. At the front door I was greeted by a youth in a green blazer whom I took to be a grandson visiting for the holidays. He led me through to Crawshay who sat in his leather armchair in a small comfortable study. The youth showed me in and then, when he reached the door of the room, bowed deeply and murmured, "Master", before gliding out. He wasn't a grandson at all, he was the footman. I really had stepped into another world.

After a few minutes Crawshay asked: "Cigarette?"

"Thanks very much." Those were less health-conscious days.

A bell was pressed and the footman emerged again. He bowed. "Master?" He was asked to get cigarettes. More bowing. "Master." And so on. There was a lot more of this in the course of the next hour or two including a certain amount of kneeling down to present me with the silver milk jug as tea was served. It was one of those rare moments when I thought I was actually sitting in Welsh history, when I could see the thread stretching back a hundred and fifty years.

At the end I asked Crawshay, a genial and courteous man, if a bit on the constipated side conversationally, whether there was any problem with having such a famous and resonant name.

"Oh yes," he said. "Everyone thinks you're frightfully rich."

The point about all this, from Colonel Crawshay to Windsor Williams's father, is that, although the subtleties of class would have eluded an outsider's casual glance, this was a society in which people understood their relationship with each other and with the rest of the world. You knew how it worked even if one of your chief objectives in life was to overthrow it, a condition which gave rise to a society which was, above all, politically radical. Glyn Williams, the South Wales Miners' President in the sixties and early seventies and a leading figure in the Labour Party nationally, once explained ruefully: "When I go to London, they think I'm the red menace. Down here, I'm a right-winger."

No wonder when the present Prince of Wales visited Aberaman a disgusted voice came from among the spectators: "Look at him. What does he know? He's wearing a three-piece suit and slip-on shoes." So much for those who think that people in the South Wales valleys consider the ultimate in formal clothing is wearing a baseball cap the right way round.

It's difficult as well to over-estimate the dismay felt in the men-only club of industrial strife when women started poking their noses in. Their involvement in the long, futile and ultimately disastrous strike of 1984-85 was publicly applauded and privately resented. It was as if the Beverley Sisters had turned up in the College of Cardinals, and clearly another vile consequence of the triumph of Margaret Thatcher.

When it was all over, lots of other things were supposed to be over too. "They can get back in the kitchen where they belong," growled one senior figure in the NUM. But they weren't going.

And as for homosexuals – *well*. When the Welsh MP Leo Abse was piloting through the Commons the reform which became the Sexual Offences Act of 1967, he had to use all his considerable reserves of guile and tenacity to get majorities in the necessary votes. In the final stages of the Bill he had to ensure that there were a hundred supporters in the House throughout the night so that it wouldn't get filibustered out of existence.

The Welsh mining MPs owed Abse a favour because he'd previously assisted on a measure to help sufferers from pneumoconiosis. Abse knew the miners well enough. They were totally opposed to any liberalisation of the laws on homosexuality so he persuaded them to keep away. "They had an obligation to me," he told me twenty years later. "I was able to say to them: 'Take the miners' MPs away. If you come, don't vote.' And the Welsh miners' MPs took the other miners' MPs home."

Why miners should take such an illiberal attitude has been the subject of much psychological speculation over the years. Is it the fear of people working in an environment with enough symbolism to make a Freudian analyst light up with anticipation? An all-male occupation carried out in the half light of tunnels far below ground... who needs to go on? The question that follows is whether they fear the disruptive effect of homosexuality in such a situation, or whether they are in fact seduced at least by the idea, and so hide from that glimpse of self-knowledge?

Whatever the answer, the attitude of the miners' MPs in the sixties reflected their public certainty about the proper nature of the social order. They were people who believed in authority and discipline and the clearly defined places of men, women and children within their community. So when, in the time running up to the 1997 election, Tony Blair and Jack Straw talked about the need for measures to deal with the kind of crime and disorder that confronted people in the streets where they lived, loutish behaviour, small-scale theft, vandalism and the rest of it, they were reflecting the natural attitudes of traditional Labour supporters. While middle-class permissives now agonise with indecision over whether little Toby should go to bed before *Newsnight*, more pragmatic voters applaud demands for a child curfew and in any case impose their own.

Or they did anyway. In the house next door to us in Aberaman, for instance, you could almost tell the time by the sounds of a shouted ritual.

"Eileen," a mother would call. "Eileeeeeeen, put that bloody light out."

There would be a muffled but clearly defiant response. The stakes were raised.

"If you don't put that bloody light out, your father will take his belt to you when he gets home."

No such thing, I was assured, ever happened; violence was unknown in the household, but you can see where the former Conservative Home Secretary, Michael Howard, who was brought up in Llanelli, got his more sophisticated ideas on crime and punishment.

The problem that arises from this is that politicians, who pride themselves on their grasp of the real world and their gritty realism when confronting it, are in fact often easy marks for nostalgia. They'd quite like to go back to the idea of what these communities were like, rather than the reality, to take the good bits, the solidarity, the sense of belonging, the interdependence, those qualities which flourish vigorously in the greenhouse of the political imagination.

A really big brain could see at once how readily this might be achieved. In 1987 Peter Walker was sent to Wales as Secretary of State. Mrs Thatcher's curious valediction was ringing in his ears as he headed down the M4: "You've always been awkward, Peter, but perhaps I need someone awkward in Wales." Or even further away, if that were possible, is the unspoken comment most of us would have detected.

Walker was a man with a genius for self-promotion but little sense of irony. No doubt this is why it was said that, during the composition of his memoirs, *Staying Power*, a book badly written and self-serving even by the standards of these things, the letter 'I' on his typewriter had to be replaced three times.

His view seems to have been that were was very little wrong with Wales, and the South Wales valleys in particular, that couldn't be fixed by a bit of positive thinking. And, even more important, without increasing public expenditure. So when Welsh Office civil servants offered him a choice for that year's official Christmas card he rejected them because they all had black clouds in the picture.

"I said I was not going to send all round the world pictures of Wales with black clouds. I wanted blue skies and sunshine."

And, naturally, being Walker he had a solution instantly to hand. His thirteen-year-old son Timothy had taken a photograph of the Welsh landscape on a brilliantly sunny day. "I said we would have this as our Christmas card. For the first time in the history of the Welsh Office, it had a Christmas card without black clouds."

At the same time the depth of Walker's political and economic analysis was breathtaking. "I told them I was not going to go round the world telling them Wales was depressed when it had such a magnificent landscape and other attractions." I wonder if in Cathays Park they looked on in wonder and said to each other: "Thanks, Secretary of State, if some lucky act of fate hadn't brought you here, we'd never have known that."

Equally no-nonsense and innovative was Walker's solution. "I said we were going to have to clean up the valleys and adopt a range of measures." People must have gasped in amazement. "A range of measures, eh? Is there no end to the man's brilliance?"

And so the Valleys Initiative was conceived, in itself an almost perfect piece of Government activity in that it persuaded people that something was going on without the necessity to find very much extra by way of cash. It was essentially doing what the Welsh Office had been doing for years, clearing derelict land, building advance factories and all the usual busy features of a modest programme of industrial regeneration, this time accompanied by the restless finger-clicking that characterised Walker, as did his his eye for action words like initiative.

I caught a glimpse of how this sort of thing works through my membership, at that time, of the Welsh Advisory Committee of the Design Council, a somnolent, unpaid quango. Walker decided that there should be some kind of Valleys Initiative design prize. He asked us to organise it and said in his letter: "I am willing to fund the prize" or words to that effect. Certainly the crucial word "fund" was in it. Everyone woke up and began making expensive plans, as you do in these circumstances. There'd be the necessary literature, publicity, entry forms – all professionally and expensively designed, of course – judges to be appointed, meetings to be held, lunches to be organised, a grand ceremony to be staged. I sat on this committee for many years and it was pretty well the first time we'd done anything at all.

But then we had another meeting and some of us began to smell a rat. A civil servant was asked what exactly was meant by Walker 'funding' the prize. Well, of course, the civil servant explained, surprised that we were surprised, it meant what it said. The Secretary of State would be quite happy to pay for the actual prize, the slate artefact or whatever which would appear in the photographs of him and the grateful winner. Top whack, say fifty quid. We returned to our slumbers.

I don't blame Walker because this is what politicians do, and there was no doubt that he was brilliant at it. So much so, indeed, that on one occasion he was shown on the *Nine o'Clock News* going round initiating things which, in terms of the public profile of the Welsh Office, is the media equivalent of the Nobel Prize. But one aspect of this has rather more depth, and that is the way in which the Walker episode represents the hold that the South Wales valleys have on the imagination of the outside world, the way in which they represent a kind of historical and social cohesion which can somehow be preserved, or at least reconditioned, in much the same way as old tyres are remoulded.

That Labour landslide of 1945 and the huge changes it brought didn't do it, but that didn't mean those pouring in on the next Labour landslide, that of 1997, didn't have similar ambitions. Pausing only to dismiss wheezes like the Valleys Initiative as slick marketing, New Labour invented something called the 'industrial village concept' which, you'll understand, is neither slick nor marketing. The essential idea was that modern industries, particularly those that are electronics based, should take the place of coal mining in giving the valley towns work, coherence and identity. The Nippon Widget Corporation would be the Powell Duffryn of the new millennium, perhaps.

Peter Hain, who became a junior Welsh Office Minister in 1997, arrived in Resolven from South Africa via the Young Liberals and what by then had come to pass for the left wing of the Labour Party. He was another who succumbed to that potent sense of oppression and injustice which so often shapes attitudes to present-day South Wales.

"These places were born as industrial villages when coal was discovered," he said in an early ministerial speech. "A lot of blood and sweat was shed when they acted as the energy power-house of Britain. There is a debt owing – one which in all conscience must be repaid."

Yes, yes, yes and yes again, you say when you hear people going on like this, as they often do. But these places were doomed as soon as they were built. In an extractive industry the end of production is signalled as soon as it begins, the first ton of coal that comes from the ground is the point where the graph of resources begins its inexorable downward path. Politicians, who are decent, honest and well-meaning people more often than you might think, nevertheless suffer the inevitable defect of being politicians: their belief that there are simple solutions to difficult questions; in the case of the South Wales valleys, that you can somehow retain the good and eliminate the bad. Yet it is that very combination of the good and the bad that created what these places once were and now are, and gives rise to the

romance in the first place. In any case, you can hang around on
the street corner as long as you like and kid yourself that the last
bus hasn't gone, but eventually you'll have to face up to the long
trudge home.

Windsor Williams – Duke – the grammar school boy from
Glancynon Terrace, took his father's advice – every father's
advice – and headed for what was to a previous generation the
unimaginable security of the civil service. But:

"I regretted every day of it. I got out because I couldn't face
another forty years of it. I'd have gone mental, but my mother
and father never forgave me."

Family ties drew him back to Aberaman and, as he said, he
eventually got ingrained in the valley again. "After about four
or five years you get the itch to go away and then you think,
'No', things are holding you here and you just get into the habit
and their way of life."

He set up in a carpet business more than twenty years ago.
When I went with him to his shop in Lewis Street I was
reminded of those joke sound effects on radio comedy
programmes where chains are rattled, bolts drawn and keys
turned, seemingly interminably. As we finally stepped through
the low doorway he told me that vandals and burglars had
finally put an end to his modest enterprise. That and the sheer
bloody awfulness of Aberaman.

"I had a friend come home the other day. He's a lecturer in
psychology in Australia. I have a few old friends who come to
see me but they all have the same attitude. 'If you want to see
me again, you come out to Australia or wherever – we're not
coming home again.' Immediately the first thought that comes
to their minds is how dirty it is, and look at it here in Lewis
Street – all the flotsam, terrible."

Inevitably Duke saw this decay as the result of neglect by
people (did I mention tribalism?) a couple of miles away up the
valley, the council.

"They haven't led this community. My sore point is that
when you go to Aberdare, to Canon Street, you'll see it all done
in lovely herringbone blocks, but Aberaman – nothing.
Aberaman has been left to die."

As we stood in his shop with the boarded up windows he

talked about a future consisting mainly, he thought, of five years on the dole, waiting for the old age pension. "I just want out, now," he said. A few months later I went back to Lewis Street to look for him, but already the shop had succumbed to the kiss of the JCB.

Doris Williams got out for a while too. She married and went to Portsmouth where she lived through the War. In 1950 the doctor said she needed a complete rest. Where else but Aberaman? But then there was a small event.

"I came back for a holiday and my sister went and got married all of a hop and I had a shop whether I wanted it or not."

She never left, although the shop – Mason's shoe shop, which had belonged to her parents – is closed now, black blinds across its window in the kind of permanent mourning that suits Lewis Street at the end of the millennium.

If you look at a place like Aberaman through the eyes of people like Windsor Williams's friends popping in from Australia, or even your own, as much a stranger as anyone after all these years, it's easy enough to be shocked and saddened by decay and dereliction. But if you live somewhere year after year the way in which it's gradually crumbling is less noticeable. Then an event comes along that jolts you with a reminder of the mortality of people and the places in which they live.

The workmen's institute (the 'stute) was the social centre of this place, along with the Grand Cinema next door. "It was where everyone went," Doris Williams said. "Everyone in Aberaman spent some part of the day or night at the institute, playing billiards, or singing, or in the reading room. The men used to gather there in the library and there was the basement where the boys used to go."

And then, in October 1994, there was a fire. Whatever they had managed to ignore previously, people were then incontrovertibly confronted by the fact that life had changed, that the social order, the relationship of people with the place in which they lived, had been overthrown, almost while they weren't looking. Essentially it was an event that made people realise how here, as in many other parts of industrial Britain, they're being separated from their history.

Doris Williams understood it well enough. "There isn't any Aberaman now, it's completely disappeared. The day the hall burnt down I cried like the rain. For me, that was the end. I stood in the garden being showered with flakes of Aberaman Hall. I don't think it was only me. It finished Aberaman for everybody."

It's not all that long ago that it was possible to go every June to the South Wales Miners conferences where even in the early seventies union officials represented almost forty thousand men. Peering through the fog of cigarette smoke that made the Porthcawl Pavilion look like the Bay of Fundy on a wet Wednesday, you could listen to the ritual denunciations of the industry itself. We will only be satisfied, someone would say to murmurs of agreement, when the last man has come up from the last pit in South Wales.

I don't know if they really wanted that to happen, certainly I don't think anyone there believed it would happen but now it more or less has, and with a speed that has left most of us breathless. It's been a disorientating process for hundreds of thousands of people as their past has been tidied away into theme parks and museums. Certainties, even hated certainties, defined people's relationship with the rest of the world. Not going down the pit, Windsor Williams's father's ambition for his son, was as much part of that definition as going down it. The pits are closed, the Aberaman Workmen's Institute has burned down, life is utterly changed, people and their history have been irrevocably parted. Only a sloganising politician unwrapping his Valleys Initiative or his Industrial Village or even, later on, the Greening of the Valleys, would think you could put them back together. But then, perhaps only a politician would want to.

Hannibal Lecter's
Schooldays

It came as no surprise to me that Sir Anthony Hopkins first achieved worldwide fame through his portrayal of a psychopath whose particular passion was for eating his victims. It must have been easy for him because, from one perspective, his role as Dr Hannibal Lecter in *The Silence of the Lambs* was little more than a heightened but well-observed version of his schooldays during the nineteen-fifties. It's true that none of the fifty boys who lived in the boarding house at Cowbridge Grammar School was ever actually discovered eating another pupil, but there were times when it must have been a close-run thing. Food, the peculiar vileness of the institutional offerings and the grudging portions in which it was served, was one of the things that shaped our lives to the point of obsession. Even now, after all this time, to bump into a Cowbridge contemporary is more often than not to fall into descriptions of notoriously disgusting meals.

"When I left Cowbridge I was six foot two and nine stone," one of them told me forty years later, as he recalled a dish known as car crash, so called because its appearance and texture suggested that it was made from the unidentifiable remains of victims brought direct from a pile-up on the A48.

Of course this was at a time, not long after the War, when genuine food shortages were fresh in people's memories. Indeed, when I went to Cowbridge in the autumn of 1952 as a particularly inadequate ten-year-old, I was clutching my ration book to enable the school to supply things like meat and butter. That was the theory, anyway, although I learnt later that the kitchen staff would regularly steal part even of the small amounts that the Government felt able to allow us.

Food was seen as a kind of privilege, an attitude shaped partly by the years of scarcity, but something that coincided as well with what was seen as the proper education of young people. It was part of our moral as well as physical nourishment. In many aspects of life the reasoning was that if we didn't like something then it was clearly good for us. If we started enjoying anything then it was a good idea to deprive us of it. Only extreme measures could break the system: one boy campaigned long and hard to be excused the grated pumice stone mixture described as porridge, but he was only successful when, sitting next to the headmaster at breakfast, he vomited his helping back into the bowl.

I realise now, although I believed otherwise then, that this regime wasn't something introduced by a malevolent administration with the chief purpose of making our lives as miserable as possible. What it represented was a particular world view which included, as it had done for generations, an acceptance of traditional physical and emotional disciplines, the imposition of which would nowadays get any teacher locked up. In one sense nineteen-fifties Britain was the last age of innocence, a time of certainties; but just because you are certain doesn't mean that you are not wrong – an axiom all too often forgotten in, for example, political life.

Because of its peculiar nature, the Cowbridge Grammar School of those days was a mirror of a certain kind of society. By modern standards it was small – three hundred and fifty boys in all and, most unusually, fifty of them in the boarding house which had been unexpectedly left over from another era. There was certainly nothing like it in the rest of the Welsh educational system. The boarders were selected from among those who had passed highest in what was still known as the Scholarship, later to become the eleven-plus, in the county of Glamorgan. It's fair to say, though, that success was not quite the achievement you might imagine since the not-so-magnificent seven who entered each year were chosen from among those whose parents actually put them forward. It was not, I suspect, a large number.

For those parents who bothered, though, I suppose it had its attractions as a kind of grammar school with knobs on, or perhaps a cut-price public school, an educational idea which had a grip on the imagination of far more people than ever went to one. Iolo Davies, a classicist who much later became headmaster, was then the senior (of only two) boarding masters.

"In the nineteen-thirties when I was in school the British Empire was here to stay. One of the other things that was here to stay was the English public school system and this trickled down to our consciousness, even to the provincial grammar schools in South Wales.

"We read twopenny papers like *The Magnet* in which the mythology of Harry Wharton and Billy Bunter and all those Greyfriars boys was the staple product. Letts' schoolboy diaries in those days had lists of irregular Greek and Latin verbs and little potted histories of English public schools like St Bees in Cumbria and all those places you'd never heard of."

Difficult though it is to credit now, the public school idea was copied in Cowbridge even down to a system of fagging in which young boys cleaned shoes and made beds for much older ones. But the really good thing from the point of view of the frugally-minded parents of South Wales was that they could get this ersatz version of St Cake's or whatever without putting their hands too deeply into their pockets. The fees were modest, since they covered only the cost of our primitive living conditions. When I arrived in Cowbridge they were, I think, about ninety pounds a year, the equivalent of a couple of thousand now. You didn't get much for that kind of money. Long afterwards Peter Cobb, who became one of the boarding masters in 1953, described the kind of place it was:

"What I remember is it being incredibly shabby, half-derelict with buckets in the top of Old Hall catching the rain, and terrible old desks steeped in history and covered with boys' carved initials. If anybody from the education system today were to go into Cowbridge as it was used for teaching, they just wouldn't believe that education could be delivered under such circumstances, and yet it was.

"The boarders had a double ration of the place because the classrooms became the evening accommodation for them and there was virtually no provision for any kind of amusement. You could play games until it got dark and there was some kind of old gramophone which you could listen to in one of the rooms, but it was lacking in any of the facilities without which I imagine a boarding house would go on strike now."

One of the most remarkable features of this way of living is that it's only by looking back that people can see how extraordinary it was to keep a small group of boys aged from eleven to eighteen, seven days a week, forty-odd weeks a year, in a building which made scarcely any concessions to their constant presence. No-one, parent, teacher, or local councillor, thought this was anything but an entirely normal way of going on. There was, for instance, not a single upholstered chair in the entire building. In effect we lived in our classrooms. There were the three dormitories in which boys slept close together on thin mattresses thrown over a wire frame. The younger boys slept at the top of the building where there was no lavatory. But at the same time they were forbidden to leave the dormitory during the night, however pressing their need. The result, inevitably, was a certain amount of bed-wetting, a cause of great shame and the object of derision rather than sympathy. But it never occurred to anyone in charge that the answer might lie in improved plumbing rather than in the grimly implied merits of self-control.

In these unsuitable domestic circumstances the prevailing mood in that great Victorian pile was not acute misery, as you might expect, but rather one of deep boredom: there simply wasn't very much to do in such spare time as the system allowed. This was a condition which I think helped increase the rate of petty crime in which most schoolboys, particularly those locked away early each evening, quickly acquire advanced skills. We did so despite the threat of another of those certainties of the age, corporal punishment, and those tempted to imagine it's an answer to present-day disciplinary problems should note that, in the way of criminals the world over, we thought we were too smart to get caught.

In fact we were, not least because the boarding masters were good natured and would, in any case, probably have found enforcing the rules conscientiously just as tedious as those on whom they were supposed to be enforced. More than that, to be fair. I bet a boy called John Bennett two shillings (10p now, a huge sum to us then) that he wouldn't go into the boarding masters' study and piss on their fire. They heard about the bet and let him do it.

Drunk boys were from time to time helped to escape the consequences of the fact that some Cowbridge publicans were perfectly happy to serve anyone tall enough to see over the counter. Unexplained absences during the long weekend evenings were not inquired into. In winter the doors were locked at six-fifteen every night so that, particularly on Saturdays and Sundays, boys aged up to eighteen or even nineteen sat around, stir-crazy, consumed by a craving for nicotine, alcohol, girls and food. In these circumstances it was perhaps just as well that the authorities clearly made a policy decision not to nail up the window through which many of us would escape for a while, sometimes several times in the course of the evening, to smoke, to drink a little British sherry perhaps or, very occasionally because of the laws of supply and demand, to take turns with one of the few eligible and compliant girls in the district. If you were more than a couple of minutes late for your date, though, someone else's hand would already be up her jumper.

In these circumstances I found, for perhaps the only time in my life, that there were some advantages to being a Catholic. In Welsh schools they like to teach Tudor history (Welsh dynasty, see, or up to a point, anyway, and certainly the best they can manage) and so, as the lone Papist in the boarding house I would annually be blamed for the burnings of Protestants by Mary Tudor as well as assorted other sixteenth-century crimes. They were arguments I came to enjoy because they helped me discover my life's vocation as a lance-corporal in the awkward squad. To this day I find being in a majority uncomfortable and ill-fitting. Nevertheless, to be a Catholic in Wales is to be reminded from time to time – even now – how thin is the gloss of tolerance over the old paint of prejudice. Many years later, when I left a restaurant table for a moment, a very senior Welsh Labour politician, a former Cabinet Minister, turned to my colleague and said that, while I was not a bad bloke, there were "too many of them about".

"Too many what?"

"Too many Irish Catholics."

My chief religious observance was hiding from the chain-smoking parish priest as he came looking for me in his Ford Popular. I would tell him that school matters had kept me away from church. I would tell teachers that the Church, whose insistent discipline they sneakingly admired, demanded my presence elsewhere. When Peter Cobb, who knew perfectly well what was going on, asked mischievously for an official, priestly, note explaining why I had been summoned to yet another religious festival, I forged one and signed it 'W. Begorrah Morris'. Nothing more was said about the matter.

Best of all, though, I went to Church on a Sunday only from half past nine until five past ten, provoking a curious mix of envy and anti-Catholicism from everyone else who had to attend Church or Chapel twice, and for long hours. While they knelt in their grey suits and stiff white collars, I smoked, listened to 'Journey Into Space' on the radio and from time to time played table tennis with a man who was later to become famous for murdering his wife.

I suppose most inmates of all institutions find accommodations of this kind. Even so, there were offences that couldn't be ignored. One boy was caught stealing food from another's tuck box (yes, tuck boxes we called them in this Woolworth's version of Harrow) and, although we were all expert at picking padlocks with the sharp points of otherwise unused geometry instruments, to steal someone else's food was the equivalent of drinking another man's water as he dozed in the drifting lifeboat.

One caning wasn't considered sufficient punishment for such an offence. The boy was sentenced to three, to be administered on successive nights. I am sorry to report that, far from this being considered an awesome object lesson, such events were a welcome contribution to our measly stock of public entertainment. Whenever a beating was imminent it was possible to rush down the corridor to a darkened classroom and, climbing on each others' shoulders like a motor-cycle formation team, peer through a clear gap in the leaded window and look across the lawn to the brightly-lit study in which the headmaster, the former rugby international Idwal Rees, would swish away stylishly, almost as if aware of his admiring audience.

Physical retribution was, though, part of the culture of the times to an extent that is unbelievable now. Tom Evans, the physics master, kept a thick piece of wood, perhaps the inside of a roller blind, with which he would occasionally beat boys for carelessness or cheek. "Face the east," he would say in preparation for a modest beating, and people somehow thought it was funny. Even when I was a sixth former, Lloyd Davies, who taught French, would pull my hair painfully in retribution for my persistent failure to make adjective and noun agree. Jim White, briefly a boarding master, would sometimes fly into terrifying rages, rampaging through the dormitories before breakfast, looking for boys to beat with a gym shoe for imagined crimes or crimes they would inevitably commit later in the day.

But what did we know of them? One evening Tom Evans left the home he shared with his mother in Gilfach Goch, walked up the mountain and slit his wrists. It was a first, distant indication for most teenagers of the tortured nature of some adult life. Jim White was a talented historian and a gifted teacher. Later, his temper cooled and, safely out of the inflammatory atmosphere of the boarding house, he guided me on how to make the best use of the small number of facts at my command, helpful for an historian and absolutely invaluable for a journalist. Sometimes, too, he would slip me a Philip Morris cigarette, his own invariable habit being to smoke only a half at any one time, something I suspect was a hangover from his days in a prisoner of war camp. The war seemed a long time ago to us, but to people like him, I thought afterwards, it must have been the day before yesterday. No wonder they behaved oddly, even violently at times.

However, when I mentioned these late-arriving sympathetic thoughts to one of these men's younger colleagues he turned out to be more cynical than we had been or even become. "Ah well," I was surprised to hear him say, "they all said that, didn't they?"

In fact the cane was used quite rarely, certainly less frequently than the dap, as the gym shoe is known in South Wales, wielded with enthusiasm by senior boys on their juniors for real or imagined offences. There is nothing to match the casual cruelties, mental and physical, inflicted in a closed society, and you can guarantee that most boys given the power to punish others will use it enthusiastically and with a sense of moral authority. Even more disturbing, perhaps, is the way in which those within such a society come to accept it on its own terms. We behave like this because we behave like this.

When I first went to Cowbridge I was told by some relatives to look out for a friend of theirs, a sixth-former who would, they said innocently, "keep an eye on me". He did. He was a boy of considerable charm, a talented actor who specialised in selling people like me things they didn't want so that, for example, although the least musical child in the whole of Wales, I was convinced that I could become a virtuoso of the mouth organ. Inevitably I never actually got beyond the first two notes of *The Blue Danube*. He would borrow money, of which there was little, and then deny that there had ever been a loan. Once you got wise to that, he would steal from you while you slept. You must have met him, he's the guy who just sold you the dud insurance policy, or the car with sand in the gearbox, occupations for which this exceptional educational experience was an invaluable training.

In this closed world the changing seasons were marked by the sounds then familiar on playing fields all over Britain: the crack of leather on cheekbone and the "oof" as knee met groin. Boarders at Cowbridge were involved in compulsory physical activity on most days of the week, something which at least meant we were kept away from the very limited sins of the flesh as were available locally. We had to play rugby, or hang around pretending to play rugby, five times a week. If the ground was so hard that life-threatening injuries were a real possibility then we were sent on a cross-country run, which some of us preferred since we were able to take our cigarettes and matches and hang around somewhere out of sight until a suitable run-length interval had elapsed.

I suppose that behind all this activity lay the theory that exhaustion was the enemy of vice, but I am surprised that even to this day the merits of compulsory sport and the character-building qualities of team games are still urged upon the public by a certain kind of politician. After all, what are most team games but organised cheating and an invitation to violence? And in the insistence on them, how many of us learned, not a spirit of interdependence to carry out into the world, but how to forge medical certificates, lie about our asthma and smoke in the back of the bus?

Naturally none of this could be explained, even admitted, to the outside world. Every Sunday morning we were obliged, under supervision, to sit down and write letters home, which meant we had to construct an alternative world for domestic consumption. We struggled to find things to say about lessons and sport and illness and the weather while at the same time concealing the reality of how we behaved and what we really thought. Old Proust, scribbling away in his cork-lined room, might have been able to write endlessly about a piece of cake, but in these circumstances I doubt if even he would have been able to get on to the second side of Basildon Bond.

In such ways we cut our ties with the world we had come from. I can't think that there was any boy there who, by the age of thirteen or fourteen, hadn't become emotionally self-sufficient. We came quickly to acquiesce in an entirely different way of life and, in the nature of existence behind high walls, we soon ceased to see anything peculiar about it, apart from a boy of genuine determination who persistently walked the twelve miles to his home in Barry until his parents had to give in and take him away. For the rest of us, the masters as much as the pupils, it was a world which had its own rules and its own individual logic, and you found a place in it as best you could.

All this might seem odd enough now, but there was another sense in which a nineteen-fifties education in Cowbridge took place in a foreign country. It arose out of the maxim we all understood: bright boys did classics. Not all of them, of course, but plenty of those who showed spark and talent. This was partly a reflection of the fact that the headmaster was himself a classicist, but it was by no means extraordinary in a grammar school of those times and, as you might guess, it certainly reflected the contemporary public school ethos.

"If you were good enough," Peter Cobb recalled, "you did classics and if you weren't you went from history to geography to economics. In the fifties Cowbridge was thought of as being almost at the apex of education in South Wales. It was partly a residue of the days before the War when Dick Williams was headmaster and flogged them all through their classics and there were some very brilliant achievements." And he meant flogged.

This doesn't mean that boys couldn't do the sciences or that they didn't do so successfully. But the teaching of even something as basic to modern education as biology didn't take its place in the curriculum until the mid-fifties. And that was in the

46

context of a school where, in order to manage the great Welsh surname famine, people were given Latin numbers to distinguish them. So there were people like Williams Tertius, Quartus, Quintus, Sextus and the rest of the Williamses, or even someone called Davies Undevicesimus – Davies Nineteen as we translated him – who was by no means the last of his numbered tribe.

There was too another aspect to our identities which marks that out as a time and a place that, from here, now, simply seems exotic. Despite the confusions that could arise, we were more often than not known to the teachers and each other by our surnames. Social change is such now that, although when I call someone by his surname I do so as a sign of affection and intimacy, in the modern world it is often taken as a patronising and so rather offensive form of address.

That's only one minor change which makes it clear today that in Cowbridge Grammar School in the nineteen-fifties we were living in a particularly ramshackle part of the folk museum that was the post-war British education system, something underlined by the famous 1944 Education Act. Once a Labour government had been elected in 1964 it was doomed, although in many places the grammar school struggled on for a long time, not least in Cowbridge where Iolo Davies fought bitterly against Labour councillors to keep it alive.

It would be wrong, though, to assume that it was politics which was entirely responsible for the new order of things. Politicians and their parties are often breathlessly running after the tail lights of social change, wise after the event, claiming that they've been saying all along what people have managed to work out perfectly well for themselves. It's long been fashionable to identify the sixties as the decade of dramatic change, but young people emerged into that daylight dragging sex and rock 'n' roll and sedition with them. You can hear it, as you often can, in the music. Bill Haley, Chuck Berry and, above all, Elvis Presley, every mother's nightmare, every boy's role model. Iolo Davies picks out in particular the open defiance, the literal revolution, of *Roll Over Beethoven*.

"*Roll Over Beethoven* was an expression of revolt. Pupils didn't just want to accept anything on a plate any more" Iolo

Davies said. "You had to justify it. This was when people began to grow their hair long just to prove they could grow their hair long if they wanted to and that there wasn't any schoolmaster who was going to stop them doing it."

Out of the way, Beethoven, you're finished, Beethoven, you and the rest of square scene, is what Chuck Berry meant when he sang: "Roll over, Beethoven – tell Tschaikowsky the news." American popular culture was suspect then, as it is to some people now, but it can't be a coincidence that 1956, when that song was written, was in Britain the year of John Osborne's play, *Look Back in Anger* and the emergence of the cult of the angry young man.

"All those pied pipers ran away with the kids in about 1956 and that was a kind of musical youth revolution that started then and has been going on ever since."

Iolo Davies told me all this and much more something like forty years later, in a tone of dissatisfaction, of disappointment with the world, which I think I was able to detect even all that time ago behind the broadminded, genial, scoutmasterly manner in which he went about the small world of Cowbridge, walking like a sailor, his shoulders swinging from side to side, his round eyes swivelling in time with them.

He was everything a schoolmaster ought to be, dedicated, tolerant, inventive, inspiring to those he taught. He was even relaxed enough to lend me his car one Sunday, against all the rules you could think of, so that I and another sixth former could escape for a couple of hours. In an astonishing piece of enterprise year after year he produced *The Lion*, a magazine which every weekend would be written by him and a team of boys and which he would then type out and print on a Gestetner duplicator in time to be sold for a penny to the day boys arriving on Monday morning. Who would do such things now? Who else would have done such a thing even then?

Yet behind this dedication to schoolmastering it was possible even then to get a sense of discontent, of depression, of melancholy, that somehow, for all its satisfactions and challenges, life wasn't really what it ought to be. And at the same time, for all his liberal attitudes in personal relationships, there was also a sense of disapproval of those who didn't describe the world as he saw it. Or, perhaps, less disapproval than disappointment.

He was in his mid-seventies when I went to see him in his tiny flat in Cheltenham ("You'll never find it," he said gloomily on the phone), a volume of Thucydides open by his chair, understanding why the days of Cowbridge Grammar School, and other places like it, had eventually had to pass, but regretting nevertheless the folly of those who had brought that about.

"Education was seen as though it were a personal advantage handed out to young people. Quite understandably, the majority of parents whose sons weren't going to county schools – because they hadn't passed the Scholarship – said education was a social advantage which their children should get, that everybody should have.

"You might say that's perfectly just and that's the principle on which we try to work now. Some people say that the result is what the Americans call dumbing down of our culture. It's not for me to say. I'm not in the teaching game now, so it's up to other people to judge but education has become, as the phrase used to be, social engineering."

In among those disclaimers you cannot fail to hear the regret, and even at the end of the twentieth century Iolo is by no means alone in that. But perhaps even in the fifties, despite whatever education might have become, what was clear was that the kind of change represented so noisily by rock 'n' roll would find expression in more significant ways as people questioned the particular social order it underpinned.

"College cocks, twopence a box," town boys would sometimes shout derisively at us, a reference to our school badge of three cockerels over the motto *Vigilis et Virtute*, and by doing so emphasised the class divide institutionalised in the education system. It didn't mean that if you were poor you couldn't get to the grammar school – many town boys were fellow pupils – but if you failed, it was the secondary modern school for you, a place where academic ambition was specifically discouraged.

In a slightly more subtle way you could see this even within the grammar school itself. The forms were numbered conventionally – IIa, IIb, IIIa, IIIb (Roman numerals, natch) and so on until you got to the fifth form. Then it was Va for one lot but, for the second stream, Vm. M? M for modern, in a world where the battle between the new and the old, the classical world and the twentieth century, ancient and modern, was somehow always won by the guys with the spears and shields rather than the ones with the tommy-guns and Sherman tanks. Despite the scientists in the 'A' forms, some of whom went on to distinguished careers, modern was still a boo word, a hold-your-nose word, in a sense an indication of comparative failure.

The place to be in those days was not just in the grammar school but in its 'A' stream where you were doubly chosen, something which in its turn meant the vast majority of the population was officially designated as second rate. There was only a small amount of movement between A and B forms and hardly anyone managed to get a second chance by transfer from the secondary modern. Most of those who were not chosen in that fatal week at the age of eleven had the educational path of their lives set and, with it, the economic and social courses too.

It's difficult to believe that people, the voters, would have stood for such a system much longer if it had not been dismantled voluntarily. Far more people were made aware of their freedom by rock music than were driven on to the streets by the *Communist Manifesto*, and it was perhaps one of the key influences in making them challenge accepted structures and received wisdom and assert their rights instead.

In these circumstances it's futile to argue whether one system is or was better than another. Education has changed because it had to change and when people talk, as John Major did as recently as 1997, of "a grammar school in every town that wants one," you might as well talk about resuming the practice of sending small children up chimneys. You can't study Greek at a single state school in Wales and there can't be many which teach Latin. Corporal punishment has gone; even using a loud voice and a threatening gesture could land a teacher in court. You can't, I'm told, make children take part in sport and, where once a parent would ask anxiously, "What's little Darren been doing wrong?" now he's more likely to demand, "What have you been doing to my little Darren?"

Oh well, *Tempora mutantur et nos mutamur in illis*, we might have been able to translate forty years ago, times change and we change with them. Now, though, even senior civil servants and judges are being told not to use Latin tags of that kind because they make them seem remote from real life.

In all this I think the story of Tony Hopkins, who might well have been a contender for the title of most hopeless schoolboy in Wales, has a particular relevance. I once told one of his biographers, to be gentle, that we'd called him 'Mad' Hopkins to distinguish him from various other Hopkinses in the school, but the truth is that we did think he was crazy and I think he thought so himself.

"I just didn't get it," he told me years later. "I just didn't understand what to do."

Even among the disaffected spirits of the boarding house, of whom I considered myself to be a player of international standard, Hopkins was clearly, even then, world class. Not as a rebel, but as a kind of non-participant in life around him. Not unfriendly, but not particularly social, a bit taciturn, perhaps, certainly isolated. If he didn't understand the school, though, we didn't understand him as he spent much of his time slumped over the battered upright piano in the schoolroom, playing music of shattering melancholy which he might or might not have composed himself.

When Hopkins began to make a name for himself as an actor, Idwal Rees could be heard to say with some astonishment: "Do you know that boy never made a single appearance on any stage while he was in school here?"

The implication seemed to be that Hopkins knew all along that he was a brilliant actor and was deliberately concealing the fact in order to put one over on the school authorities and in general display what we then called a bolshie character. Teachers usually assume, not unjustly, that their pupils occupy a great deal of their waking lives getting away with something. Even so, it never seemed to occur to Rees that for a number of years he lived close to Hopkins in a small community of which he was in charge and that he might therefore have made a bit of an effort to find out something more about him. He might possibly have discovered that part of Hopkins's character which led him, when he left school with one 'O' level, to go and do some amateur acting at the Port Talbot YMCA so that, as he said, "I could get a bit of self-confidence."

In a sense, though, this is to miss the point. If Hopkins had been the sort of tractable chap who thought it would be fun to give the school play a bit of a bash, then he almost certainly wouldn't have become the compelling actor he has proved to be on stage and in films. On the few occasions I've spent any time with him since I've always felt that I can recognise the boy I once knew (although really only in the middle distance) in the man I've seen since, including the quirks and the well-chronicled torments.

What is both fascinating and cheering is the thought that, from here, it's possible to see that probably Cowbridge didn't really make any difference to him, or indeed to any of us except in so far as it provided a certain amount of knowledge and technique with which to approach yet another exam. In the case of Hopkins, of course, that amounted to virtually zero. We all became, as he did, what we were going to become anyway. I thought it was a terrible place, an oppressive place, and I went on thinking that, perhaps I still think that, but I now also know that it was a view that said as much about my particular condition as it did about the endless absurdities and occasional cruelties of the system.

Iolo Davies, grumbling away in Cheltenham, Thucydides by his side, was one illustration of the persistence of the individual character. So, too, was Peter Cobb, who got married, gave up schoolmastering and Methodism, became a Church in Wales clergyman and, at seventy, seemed as much at ease with life as he had always been. Decades later he recalled my own place in that closed society which he described as "shouting discouragement from the sidelines". It's true enough and, when you think about it, it didn't need much adaptation to turn it to practical use in a working life spent in various forms of journalism.

"Surely we're the same all our lives," Cobb said, "and as we get older we're just the same – but even more so."

Necking on the Railings

The twentieth century took its time getting to Aberystwyth. I was there when it arrived, actually, in October 1960. Until that time the most daring things that had been seen in the English department of the University College of Wales were Professor Gwyn Jones's suede shoes, something that marked him out as a dangerously raffish figure. I am a writer as well as an academic, the footwear announced, a creative intelligence as well as a particular expert on Old Icelandic, although that latter talent was by itself enough to tell you what sort of operation he ran. The key to any kind of progress in the department was proficiency in Anglo-Saxon and, although in the first year there was a nod at the contemporary world through the study of a volume of Welsh short stories (edited by Gwyn Jones himself, as it happened), the sixteenth and seventeenth centuries were considered to be quite up-to-date enough for people who weren't, in those days, even old enough to vote.

At that time, though, as that momentous decade began, in an unprecedented spasm of intellectual adventure, the department introduced a course in modern literature. In the space of a single summer vacation it leapt forward more than a thousand years from the impenetrable mysteries of the *Anglo-Saxon Chronicle* to the work of authors you might just have bothered to read because you wanted to. Some of them were exotic figures, too, Americans like Hemingway and Faulkner, people who were still alive, for heaven's sake. There was even D.H. Lawrence, a writer whose name alone was enough to turn an entire Nonconformist congregation rigid with outrage – in particular at that specific moment in history.

Terry Hawkes, a Shakespeare scholar who was later to become a professor of English in Cardiff, was one of the young assistant lecturers drafted in to teach this stuff. He recalled that the change the new course represented in Aberystwyth itself reflected, more or less coincidentally, something that was happening on a more dramatic scale in the outside world.

"As the term opened in my first job in October 1960, that

was the very month that the *Lady Chatterley* trial opened. There was this parade of Eng. Lit. experts being questioned by a learned judge as to the value of a novel and there I was in Aberystwyth, doing something similar and feeling very much in tune with the times. When I say the twentieth century began in 1960, there's a sense in which it did. The world we now regard as contemporary or modern began then."

The ostensible argument in the prosecution of *Lady Chatterley's Lover* concerned its explicit sexual descriptions and the repeated use of words which most of us had at that stage never seen in print anywhere, never mind in a Penguin book. The defence was that literary merit overrode the need for the state to protect a suggestible public from the consequences of, it was implied, filth. Looking back from a time when four-letter words routinely appear in the pages of the serious newspapers it's difficult to recall how innocent we were then, not simply in terms of what was considered fit for the rest of us to read, but also in understanding what the fuss was really all about.

That was contained in a single famous question put to the jury by the prosecuting counsel, Mervyn Griffith-Jones. "Is it a book," he asked, "you would even wish your wife or your servants to read?"

Now even in 1960 that was a pretty anachronistic thing to say. Most wives, if not all of them, decided for themselves what they were going to read, and servants were by then virtually unknown, except in the homes of the very rich. But Griffith-Jones, a bit late in the day admittedly, revealed in a few words that the trial was about class as much as it was about sex, always an explosive mixture in British life and both subjects which, despite everything, continue to obsess us. What that question really proposed was that, by allowing the book to be sold freely and legally, the jury would in effect be endorsing adultery between their servants and their wives. People should ask themselves where such a social upheaval might end. The question, like the trial itself and the acquittal of *Lady Chatterley*, was one of the trumpets in the fanfare that announced the arrival of the sixties, a decade which, even stripped of the myths which have grown up around it, changed all our lives comprehensively.

In the autumn of 1960, though, I suppose Mervyn Griffith-

Jones's question might not have seemed quite as outlandish in Aberystwyth as it did in literary London. We were moving slowly into the light, something you can detect, I think, in the transition from being undergraduates, a sort of flannel bags term, to being students, a much more demotic word. Despite that, though, many of us were unbelievably decorous, so much so that we might have been our own parents. We smoked and drank, naturally, but so did many of them. Some of us frequently wore ties and check sports coats, and even dinner jackets for big meetings of the debating society in which we aped the conventions of the Oxford and Cambridge Unions. Rock 'n' roll might never have been heard of as we shuffled or stumbled to the three-four time of the Les France dance band in the parish hall on Saturday nights. On the big occasions, two or three times a year, the students' union splashed out on a star attraction – Joe Loss, perhaps, or Ted Heath, and their Titanic-style bands. In some ways it might just as well have been 1912.

Deian Hopkin, who went to Aberystwyth as a student in the sixties and then stayed for more than twenty years as a history lecturer, had very much the same impression. "I think the most striking image in my mind is people going to be fitted out for gowns so that they could wear them in lectures, and for formal meals in their halls of residence. Then they signed in and out of their halls of residence and took part in all those rituals which were very redolent of the forties and fifties, and I think were a close historical link to the twenties and thirties. I could talk to my aged aunt and we would compare notes. To a large extent it was the same Aberystwyth."

There was, as Deian Hopkin recalled, a college song book. There was even a college song, – no, really.

It went, I think:

> O, College by the Sea,
> What may your motto be?
> *Nid byd byd heb wybodaeth*
> Answer we.

Did we really sing that? Not often, I suspect, although our collective sense of the ridiculous was perhaps not as highly developed as it should have been. But we did sing a lot, in pubs on Saturday evenings, before debates in the exam hall, hymns in Welsh and English, medleys including numbers like *Down by the Riverside* and *Me and My Gal*, and some songs of which we scarcely knew the meaning. One of the most popular was the Italian anti-fascist anthem, *Avanti Populo*, with its dramatic last verse which was whispered until the final, shouted, denunciation of Mussolini. Il Duce might have been dead for fifteen years or so by that time, but he still had a useful function to perform when it came to establishing students' radical credentials. Many years later I joined in once more at a Labour Party conference where Neil and Glenys Kinnock (who'd learnt it in Cardiff) were still singing it, and giving it all they'd got, which was plenty. In a cruel put-down at one of these occasions, Kinnock turned to me and said: "You sing worse than Michael Foot." True of course, despite all that practice in Aberystwyth, but there was no need to say it.

And then there was sex. Or, rather, there wasn't. Every night, in that critical, passionate half hour that was the interval between the pubs closing and curfew being sounded in the women's halls of residence, hundreds of couples would line the landward side of the promenade for some form of coastal, non-mating, wildlife ritual. There was a kind of protocol which meant that women had their backs to the railings and men theirs to the Irish Sea, thus gallantly protecting their escorts from the worst effects of the prevailing westerlies. There, for thirty minutes, the couples would kiss passionately. Anything much more than kissing, amid the clashing toggles of damp duffel coats, was difficult to achieve. This nightly extravaganza was known, with stark literalness, as necking on the railings.

If I hadn't been there, if I hadn't seen it, if I hadn't done it, I would be disinclined to believe that was how people once behaved. But it was so much a part of our lives that no-one found it in any way peculiar. Indeed, one evening when I was busily engaged in the usual not-very-much, the historian Gwyn A. Williams stopped by for a minute or two to give me an extremely useful hint about an examination paper he had set and which I would be sitting the following day.

I'm not trying to say that no-one ever listened to Elvis Presley or that, given the ingenuity and libido of the average student, sexual intercourse never took place, but it was a less casual and less accepted part of life than it was to become quite soon – "Between the end of the *Chatterley* ban / And the Beatles first LP," as Philip Larkin was to put it. Girls who became pregnant disappeared silently from our lives, rather than parking the baby buggy outside the lecture room, as they might now.

It was only as the result of a piece of unprecedented civil disobedience a few years before, a student strike no less, that a concession which allowed men to visit women in their hostel rooms for a couple of hours on Saturday and Sunday after-noons had been wrung from the authorities. This wasn't considered much of a risk, I suppose, because staff were on the premises, alert for the squeak of bedsprings. In any case the devout majority of the college council knew, as did all serious chapel-goers, that sexual intercourse did not take place during the hours of daylight.

In fact Aberystwyth had experimented with the modern world briefly and disastrously a few years before. In 1953 the College had appointed as principal Goronwy Rees, a Fellow of All Souls, a journalist, a wartime army officer, Aberystwyth-born and a son of a particularly distinguished Nonconformist Minister. The trouble was that he fitted into his new job like a bottle of scotch at a meeting of the Band of Hope. He was cosmopolitan, liberal, fond of drink, often short of money and by all accounts had a persistently energetic sex life: in short he possessed most of the characteristics which have come to be associated in particular with the lifestyle enjoyed by many sons of the manse who in these matters often strike you as people who think they've got something to prove. We should remem-ber, too, that unseemly behaviour is by no means unknown within the manse itself, or so I am told.

Later Rees was to write in *A Chapter of Accidents*, one of his volumes of autobiography, of his astonishment at the absence of student protest even then, the way in which "they accepted almost without question the rule of primitive methodism imposed on them by the college administration". And on his own return he reflected ruefully: "I would have been wiser if I had understood that at Aberystwyth I was re-entering a society far more primitive than any which I had known for a very long time, in which nothing could be taken at its face value and everything had to be interpreted in terms of conflicts that were fought on some much lower level than the rational."

Rees's arrival was in a sense to dramatise the struggle between the forbidding puritanism of the Aberystwyth orthodoxy (and by extension that of the rest of rural Nonconformist Wales) and the agnostic world of reckless self-indulgence which was threatening to overwhelm it. On Saturday mornings he drank in the back bar of the *Belle Vue Royal Hotel* with young lecturers. The more rigid members of the college staff and council, of whom there were plenty, sniffed with disapproval as Rees and his cronies strolled laughing on to the promenade in the lunchtime air.

As revealing as anything about this period was the question Rees was later to ask himself. It was "... what kind of person the Principal of the College should be? Should he be one who put the pursuit of knowledge above the preservation of the Welsh language, reason above Nonconformity, lowered his dignity by making friends with students and junior lecturers, was not greatly concerned with their morals as long as they did their work, and even helped to corrupt them by offering them a drink when he invited them to his house?"

Such an exotic figure with such extravagantly liberal ideas was doomed in nineteen-fifties Aberystwyth. The forces of repression were bound to get him, although they did so in an unexpectedly sensational manner. It is described by Rees himself in *A Chapter of Accidents* and by his daughter Jenny whose book, *Looking for Mr Nobody*, published in 1994, was an attempt to pin down the truth about the more elusive aspects of Rees's life and character.

Long after his death in 1979, speculation persisted that Rees had been a spy, a Soviet agent of some kind. Before the war he was familiar with that world, maybe more, in particular through his close friendship with Guy Burgess, the British diplomat who fled from Britain with Donald Maclean in 1951 when warned by Kim Philby that they were about to be unmasked as Soviet agents.

The two men went to the Soviet Union but it was not until

five years later, in February 1956, that they made their first public statement about their defection, at a press conference in Moscow. It was at last a clear confirmation that they were Communist agents, something which until then, Rees records, he had been trying to convince himself was not true. Until they popped up in Moscow he had clung to the idea that they were in hiding in Algeria and to him their action was a shocking personal betrayal too.

The following month *The People* newspaper began the publication of a series of anonymous articles on Burgess of which the publicity material trumpeted: "His closest friend speaks at last." The unnamed author was also described as "... Burgess's closest friend for more than twenty years and [who] now occupies a high academic post." To say the least it was a piece of astonishing naiveté on Rees's part to believe he could keep his identity a secret – perhaps, indeed, he didn't think he could but was reckless enough not to care – and it was only a couple of weeks before *The Daily Telegraph* named him as the author.

As MI5 agents turned up at Plas Penglais, the Principal's residence in Aberystwyth, to make further inquiries, the scandal broke, inflamed beyond Welsh establishment measure by Rees's descriptions of Burgess's promiscuous homosexuality and the allegations that there were traitors still at the heart of British life. Indeed there were, including Philby and Blunt, as we were to discover later. It was the opportunity the anti-Rees faction, a very substantial group, had been waiting for.

The College President, Sir David Hughes-Parry ("A distinguished lawyer of impeccable virtue, a dull mind and ardent Welsh patriotism," according to Rees) asked him to go quietly, in which event everything would be made as easy as possible. It was an offer Rees found himself able to refuse. He fought the attack on him and appeared to win. But the opposition was simply gathering its forces together. A committee of enquiry (all three members were imported from England) was established. It investigated diligently into 1957. When it eventually finished its work the committee could find no fault with Rees personally or in his conduct of college affairs. Frustratingly unable to attach blame somewhere, it fell back on generalised disapproval and described the *People* articles as "a lewd document".

The message, Rees thought, was clear enough. It was "... a phrase so heavy with moral and legal implications that it was in itself sufficient to indicate their belief that I was not a proper person to be Principal of the college." Worse, the committee was shocked that Rees's wife had typed the articles. "The report implied that my wife had connived at some particularly distasteful form of literary obscenity."

The Principal, who had made up his mind to resign in any case, left Aberystwyth which was thus saved, for the time being at least, from some of the most sordid manifestations of the modern world outside.

Not for all that long, as it turned out, but even then the kind of revolution which was to come to Aberystwyth was a watereddown Welsh version. A bit of a change, all right, but nothing too sudden or too daring. In Wales's most emphatic word of praise, tidy.

"I remember people protesting on a Saturday night," Deian Hopkin told me, "because they didn't want any more live dance band music. They wanted Beatles records and I think that was a major change. In 1965 they threw their gowns away and people began to stand for the student union presidency under political labels." Even so, when students finally took to the streets, they didn't do so to tear down the fabric of civilised society, to denounce capitalism and overthrow the oppressors. They did so in the course of an argument which even a generation ago could be conducted only in the furthest flung parts of Britain. What they wanted was to be able to drink more conveniently and more cheaply.

The question of alcohol and where you could buy it took on an almost theological character in Aberystwyth at that time. Every student was perfectly free to drink as much as they liked (although there was a theoretical prohibition on actually being drunk) in any of the thirty or so pubs in the town. What the authorities would not countenance was that they should install a bar in the students' union for the same purpose. How it must have tortured the Cardiganshire souls of the college council to see other people – publicans and sinners – making money out of their principles. This is the county, we should remember, which gets five stars in the *Good Parsimony Guide*. But the principle nevertheless remained: to permit a bar would be seen as somehow encouraging vice.

This was another illustration of the way in which in large parts of Wales, particularly the remoter rural areas, self-deception was and remains almost an industry. For example, although there are probably as many drunken people per square yard in Aberystwyth as there are anywhere else on the British mainland, the town and the surrounding district was one of the last in Wales to retain the ban on Sunday opening of pubs; but it did so in only in a notional and perfunctory manner. On one brief journalistic visit to test the prohibition I went first to the *Belle Vue*, where I was greeted warmly by the half dozen people in the back bar and was bought a beer. I then slipped along to the Conservative Club where I paid ten pence to a man who signed me in with the whispered warning, "If anyone asks, say you're a member of an affiliated organisation". Until the voters of the area finally decided in the 1989 referendum to lift the ban, the only people who found themselves obeying it were tourists, people who wouldn't have minded a half of lager. They were not only denied it, but at the same time they had to watch red-eyed locals staggering home to doze over a belated Sunday lunch.

In the mid-sixties Phil Thomas, now a professor of law in Cardiff, was president of the students' union. The clamour for a college bar was growing, particularly as the focus of academic activity moved from the town to the new campus developing on Penglais Hill, a place where there were no pubs. But when the college council considered the matter once more, the forces of reaction galloped to the rescue.

"There was an enormous response from the backwoodsmen," Phil Thomas remembered. "The Nonconformists were swept in from Plynlimon to oppose it. It was very much like the House of Lords on a tough day when the old Tory peers are brought in. There was this unholy alliance between these sectarians and the commercial interests in the town itself. The publicans were afraid that the heavy drinking which characterised the male student population would go to the students' union itself and, of course, the profit would also go in that direction."

The intransigence of the college authorities provoked a strike, called by Phil Thomas and the executive of the Students' Representative Council. "There was a total walkout on the day. We marched up and down the prom and members of the student executive all put on their robes. I was dressed in desert boots, cavalry twill trousers of a biscuit colour, check shirt, tweed hacking jacket, knitted tie, Buddy Holly glasses and a Meerschaum pipe. When you think about the idea of flower power and blue jeans and so forth, these hadn't reached a significant proportion of the people of Aberystwyth who adopted their own radical style."

Eventually the bar was established, something that now certainly, perhaps even then, could be seen as a rather trivial event, the kind of argument that, virtually as soon as it's over, leaves both sides wondering what the fuss was about. Phil Thomas, though, sees it as being more significant in a sort of Aberystwyth-altered way.

"In a sense I think this was a turning point in how students saw themselves. Perhaps the cause itself was not something we could reflect on as being an important cause in terms of Vietnam or CND and what went on subsequently, but I think it gave students a sense of their own power and perhaps their own worth. In a way I look back on it as a turning point in student policy, student aggression, student flexing of what they could and could not do.

"Traditionally, student politics in Aberystwyth would involve the student executive being invited to the Principal's office at the beginning of the year where they would have tea and biscuits and be told firmly the way in which they were expected to behave. Then they were dismissed and got on with it. I think this was a confrontation which had never occurred previously and it took the university authorities very much by surprise. They never thought we would go as far as we did."

It may not seem like much at this distance, but it does represent an important strand in what we can now see was a rapidly changing British society. The politicisation of the student class was one aspect of this, and Aberystwyth was to be instrumental in giving it a Celtic twist. While radical young people around the country, around the world, were turning to the Trotskyite factions and international socialism, some of their counterparts in Wales looked inwards and to the past. So Aberystwyth was one of the places where the Welsh language campaigns began, campaigns that were in many ways the most energetic and most successful manifestation of political activism in post-war Wales.

Their beginnings were modest enough. In 1962, Gareth Miles, later a trade union official and now a writer, fought for legal processes to be made available in the Welsh language by ostentatiously riding round the town with someone on the cross-bar of his bike. Eventually even the Cardiganshire police could look the other way no longer and he was summonsed. He refused to pay the fine because the summons wasn't in Welsh and in consequence he was arrested and taken to court. The matter was resolved briskly (and in Welsh, of course) but it was more than a modest gesture. Language activism was no interest of mine, but a friend urged me to go to the court with him because he recognised, rightly, that this was not a piece of transient eccentricity but the beginning of a campaign which has now been running for more than thirty years.

It has had darker aspects. At the same time as the bicycle incident Emyr Llewellyn, another Aberystwyth student, was planning the bomb at the Treweryn reservoir which was to get him a year in gaol. As we were to find out, the language campaigns were a mixture of the daft, the shrewd and the dangerous, but we shouldn't underestimate the brilliance with which many of them have been conducted. In particular they've had an impressive strike rate in forcing embarrassed authorities to admit the error of their ways, something which even the least subversive of us must surely find cheering.

Deian Hopkin, who as well as being an Aberystwyth academic was also a Labour politician from a family of Labour politicians, watched these events unfold. "The growth of Welsh national consciousness was certainly very visible even in the early sixties in Aberystwyth. I think it's part of the Welsh Nonconformist cultural tradition, something which grew naturally out of it. It was an opportunity to be heroic with a good historical legitimacy. I think it's interesting that the forms of rebellions Welsh-speaking Wales adopted were so different from those adopted by their English counterparts. They didn't rebel by going for an amoral society, they went for highly moral high ground politics instead."

At the same time it was possible to detect a significant social shift, notably in our relationships with the people who taught us. In general there was a huge gulf between students and academic staff, our attitudes to each other largely reflecting a continuation of the teacher-pupil axis with which we were familiar from school. The history department, to which I was most closely connected, had at its head a man called Reginald F. Treharne, a portly Mancunian who had been a professor in Aberystwyth since 1930 and who was most notable for having published no academic work of any kind for at least a quarter of a century.

Such figures of stupendous authority didn't really seem like human beings to most of us and there was some surprise in the department when it was reported that Treharne had made a joke, the only one ascribed to him in his long career in Aberystwyth. On an occasion when he was confined to his house by a back injury, some of his students had to go there for tutorials. "Ah," he greeted them, "you will see that the Chair of history has now become the Bed of history."

Final year students were occasionally obliged to attend grim Sunday evenings in that house in Cliff Terrace, desperately trying to make some kind of relevant conversation without any assistance from tobacco or alcohol. Mrs Treharne, a magistrate who was a particular scourge of motoring offenders, would bring things to a close with the serving of what she called "my special ice cream", an impossibly rich confection made with syrups and cream and who knows what else, which challenged even the few present who didn't have the usual Sunday hangover. It was part of our folklore that one student, overcome by nausea, had taken advantage of the brief absence from the room of both Treharnes, and been sick behind the sofa.

So cringingly awful were these social events that it became widely assumed that the character of the appalling Professor Welch, another historian, in Kingsley Amis's book *Lucky Jim*, which had been published in 1954, was based on Treharne. This rumour had no substance, but the film of the book became very popular in the college, perhaps because history students in particular treated it as a documentary rather than a work of fiction.

At the same time, though, the history department also contained subversive elements like the astonishing Gwyn A. Williams, five foot one of undiluted brilliance, radical outlook, magnetic charm and explosive temperament, and Richard Cobb, who was later to become Professor of Modern History at Oxford and recognised as one of Europe's most distinguished historians. (He had also been one of Goronwy Rees's Saturday morning drinking companions.)

He lived in Paris during the vacations and in the *Belle Vue* during term. Or at least he did so until he was expelled after an unfortunate late night incident at which I was present, involving drink, for which he had something of a weakness, and a girl who had decided "to save Richard from himself". This was something girls tried to do more often than you might imagine, particularly given the fact that Richard was rather weedy-looking, pop-eyed behind his thick glasses, a sort of school swot figure but entertaining, compassionate, subversive and funny. We recognised his qualities even then but it was only much later, reading his volumes of memoirs, that I realised, in one of those infuriating insights of middle age, how much of him I'd missed.

I didn't learn anything like enough from people like Richard and Gwyn and others, but one thing did emerge clearly enough from their work and teaching, something which has since had a particular importance in Wales, as we shall see. That was the then novel idea that history didn't actually stop dead at 1282 or 1543 or 1649 or 1707 or whenever. It turned out, sensationally, that history might also concern itself with the study of events within reach of our own times and that it might even reveal something of our present condition. History didn't have to be, shouldn't be, a chronicle of kings and queens and prime ministers, but a description of the people.

Even more important at the time was the idea that some of the people who taught us were essentially very much like us. They were witty, passionate, gossipy and keen to socialise. And, of course, they were young. Terry Hawkes, for example, was not all that much older than his students. "There was a matiness about it," he recalled, "and of course you could never escape from the university. If you went to a pub or a restaurant you met students – your own students, and that was lovely." This breaking down of barriers between the teachers and the taught was just the particular way in which that university responded to what was a general trend in society. It was a sort of egalitarianism, although perhaps a deceptive one: just because we now live in a society in which virtually everyone is on first name terms with everyone else, it doesn't mean that there are no structures, no pips and stripes. But this was one of the influences under which young people began to distrust hierarchies, traditions and authority, the idea that someone knew better than you because they were older, more experienced or held a position of power and influence.

You can mark that out in some of the events of the time. *Beyond the Fringe* opened at the Edinburgh Festival in 1960, providing a model for the subversive and iconoclastic comedy that followed in various forms. *Private Eye* began publishing in 1962. The BBC launched *That Was The Week That Was* in a short-lived rush of satire which had the curious effect of undermining the image and authority of the very institution which paid to put it on. Suddenly there was a licence to mock and challenge and expose. Some people think the revolution of the sixties was concerned with sex, but it was more than that: it was about attitude. Deference was out, the age of disrespect had begun. At the time of writing, it continues to flourish.

Monty Finniston's
Flying Circus

If I had to pick a single day which marked unmistakably the passing of old, industrial Wales, then it would be February 7, 1975. That was the day on which more than a thousand men massed outside the council offices in Ebbw Vale and howled with anger at one of the people they had hitherto most admired. They jeered and booed and heckled as he struggled to make himself heard through a megaphone. "I'll tell you the truth as I've always told you the truth," he yelled, his familiar long white hair swept by the wind, but they didn't want to listen. Instead they shouted that he was a Judas.

Yet this was a man who for years had been a romantic hero of the Left, disciple, biographer and parliamentary successor to Aneurin Bevan, the district's greatest politician. He was virtually everything a man could be to become the object of worship in the South Wales valleys short of half a dozen archangels descending on the Sirhowy Valley to sweep him off to heaven in a golden chariot. Despite all that, on that day Michael Foot became, for a moment or two, a hate figure.

It was a bitter day for Foot, too. One of his most enduring characteristics has been his sense of loyalty, to people or organisations or ideas, maintained when it might have been more advantageous politically to dissemble. In his years as Ebbw Vale's MP he'd given that passion unswervingly to the cause of keeping steelmaking in the town. Now, on that Friday afternoon, he'd had to come back, as a member of a Labour Cabinet, to tell people the struggle was over. You didn't have to have much of a sense of irony to make something of the fact that at that stage he was Secretary of State for Employment.

The reason I recall this moment as marking some kind of transition in Welsh life is because, until that point, there had been a sense of unreality about the change that was sweeping through it. Yes, of course people were saying that things had to be different throughout Britain. Small, old-fashioned steelworks had to be closed. Big, new ones had to be built elsewhere if we were to have any kind of stake in the modern industrial world. But they were always saying that, weren't they, and even so nothing much happened.

Indeed, so strong was the time warp factor in the industry that, on a visit to the John Summers works at Shotton, on Deeside, in the early seventies, I was surprised when, over pre-lunch drinks, a murmur started going round. The Chairman, people said, would be joining us. This was a considerable surprise, and I wondered why Lord Melchett, the head of the British Steel Corporation, was paying this unexpected visit. But it wasn't Melchett at all. The small, elderly man who arrived and was addressed as Chairman was none other than Sir Richard Summers who, four or five years before, had ridden off into the sunset of retirement, his saddlebags packed with many millions of taxpayers' pounds with which the government had bought his family business – part of the process of nationalising the industry in 1967 – the very place in which we were now drinking our gins and tonics.

This seemed to make very little difference to him. At lunch he presided at the head of the huge mahogany dining table, ladling out the salmon mousse while waitresses in white aprons poured excellent wines into the ample crystal glasses that gleamed and winked in the sunlight. 1971? It might just as well have been 1871. As I looked down the table at Sir Richard, a thought crossed my mind. A few years before his death in 1970, the Portuguese dictator, Dr Antonio Salazar, had a severe stroke and had to be replaced as head of the Government. However, it was said that people were so afraid of him, even in his enfeebled condition, they preferred not to let him know he was no longer in charge. In the same way, had the people who ran Shotton, nervous of the consequences, been unwilling to explain to Sir Richard Summers that he was in fact no longer the chairman of a private company?

It was just possible. Not literally so, perhaps, but this small incident represented the way in which things change and don't change at one and the same time. Even years after nationalisation there was a very powerful sense of the past in some of those works, ghosts of ironmasters who might drink a bottle of brandy for breakfast and then go out and oppress the workers until it was time for lunch. The facts said it wasn't going to last. Tradition, folk memory, said it would. The truth was that the scale of the problems involved was such that many people preferred to ignore them and, when they couldn't do that, to delay them by whatever means were at hand. Something might turn up, after all.

The events of that Friday in February 1975 in Ebbw Vale were especially significant because Welsh industrial history was represented in so many ways by that town. The heads of the South Wales valleys were, after all, a cradle of the Industrial Revolution. They were also the cradle of the Depression, and for nine years from 1929 the furnaces at Ebbw Vale were cold and the mills at a standstill until, against the conventional wisdom of the day, a modernised works was reopened just before the war. The town depended on its collieries, too, but the steel plant employed something like nine thousand people, a figure which, even less than a quarter of a century later, would be filed under science fiction. One measure of change is that today there can scarcely be more than a handful of manufacturing operations in the whole of Britain that employ even half that number.

In people's minds Ebbw Vale stood for the physically tough, often dangerous, labour-intensive style of work which represented industrial Wales to itself and to the rest of the world; not just South Wales, either. For such reasons it was not too fanciful to think of what was happening there as being about more than one steelworks or one town. This was the way the world was going, and it raised questions about the ability of society – governments, unions, employers, and workers – to cope with it. It also went to the core of the key political issue of ownership.

The industry had been nationalised as the last gasp of the Labour Government in 1951 and largely de-nationalised (although not Ebbw Vale, as it happened) soon afterwards. In 1967 it was taken into public ownership again, primarily as an instrument of policy, but also as a demonstration of the philosophical differences between the Labour and Conservative parties. In that sense the industry was something of a talisman. But once you control it you have to decide what you're going to do with it. And before that you have to decide, in a sense, who now owns it. Is it those employed in the industry, this being the process of securing for the workers the fruits of their labours? Or are there others, the voters, for example, who might think it's something to do with them?

In the days when I was occasionally involved in trying to teach industrialists how to present themselves on television (rarely, was often good advice), the man who ran much of the British Steel Corporation was Bob Scholey – known throughout the industry as Black Bob, a name which he claimed was derived from the colour of the hard hat he wore, but which others believed was owed to what you might call his uncompromising nature. Later, as Sir Robert Scholey, he became Chairman of the whole enterprise. Having been through the training process once he came back for a second go, admitting he was baffled.

When, for example, there was an industrial dispute in progress (when wasn't there? you could ask in those days) and he was being interviewed about it, how could he manage to address all the audiences who had a legitimate interest in its outcome? How could he reassure the workers that he had their interests at heart and was making a fair assessment of whatever their grievance happened to be? How could he, at the same time, make it clear to his managers that he had every confidence in them and wouldn't undermine their judgement and authority? How could he convince the government of the day that he was running the industry properly, with due regard for frugality and the national interest? How could he pass very much the same kind of message to the voters who were, after all, effectively the shareholders, as well as meeting the steel corporation's losses through their taxes? And how, finally, could customers have faith in his promises to cater for their needs, rather than go somewhere else for their steel?

There was no answer to this except to advise him to make regular use of expressions like 'fairness', 'firmness', and 'fine body of men'. What puzzled him were problems that arise in all industries from time to time, but which in particular go to the heart of the dilemmas posed by public ownership. Perhaps in the end this was one of the reasons the policy was eventually ditched by the Labour Party, something which, it turned out, was to have far-reaching consequences for us all.

It was not surprising that the workers at Ebbw Vale wanted to know what was the point of having a nationalised industry if it could not or would not defend their interests. They had been honest, loyal and conscientious. While other steelworks were gripped by frequent and prolonged spasms of unrest, they devoted themselves unstintingly to the success of their plant and the cause of keeping it alive.

In this they were led by the extraordinary figure of the works director, John Powell, a man who had a particular gift for inspiring loyalty and enthusiasm as well as for embarrassing people further up the chain of command in the corporation by his ceaseless promotion of the merits of Ebbw Vale. They wanted the works to give up the ghost quietly, he thumped the tub and told the world how brilliant, how efficient, how profitable it was. Not a week went by without the announcement of yet another production record from some part of the plant, something which is not as difficult as it might sound if you're the sort of person who has a creative way with statistics.

Powell was unmistakably English and enjoyed going round Ebbw Vale saying he was a Tory (Ebbw Vale is a place where sightings of Conservatives are said to be recorded in wildlife magazines). At the same time he forged a close partnership with Michael Foot who, as late as 1997, told me he still thought that Powell should have been chairman of the whole Steel Corporation. Powell organised a works rugby team in which he played (fly half, naturally) until he was well into his fifties. He had that Rank movies, wavy-haired, dashing, handsome young officer quality to which the people he led responded with enthusiasm and pleasure. It came as no surprise to learn that Major Powell had won the Military Cross during the Second World War. When he took me round the Ebbw Vale works, as he did many times, it seemed as if he were employing nine thousand public relations officers, every one of them, unprompted, urging on me the merits of the plant and its achievements.

In these circumstances it was hard to escape the feeling that, if any people deserved to keep their jobs it was these. On social grounds their argument was a compelling one, because of what the end of steelmaking would mean to the community. In the sense, too, that what they had done and were going on doing seemed to deserve some kind of reward. But at the same time there was an element of cruelty in all this because, while the workers themselves believed they could pull off the miracle, economic and industrial reality insisted that they could not. Politicians in particular misled them into believing there was an outcome possible other than closure and tantalised them with uncertainty. Years later I asked an ex-Cabinet Minister about this conflict between the clear long-term economic interests of the industry and the country as a whole, and those of the workers whose interests they as politicians were also supposed to represent. Every time, he said, it had to be the industry. I didn't believe him and all the evidence supported my view. As has so often been the case, indecision triumphed and eventually everyone paid for it.

In fact Lord Melchett, the founder Chairman of the BSC, who was to die suddenly in 1973, first announced the end of steelmaking in Ebbw Vale as early 1969. But while everyone knew the plan involved cutting the workforce by a half, some-thing Melchett had made clear to journalists in London, he claimed instead that eight thousand jobs would be protected. Many of those would be in the finishing end of the plant which would continue (as it does to this day) using steel made else-where, and many other workers could commute to the modern, Llanwern steelworks on the coast near Newport, where produc-tion was to be expanded. People were much cheered by this and preferred not to look at the figures too closely. If they had they'd have realised soon enough that they didn't add up, not least because Llanwern was a mess where the last thing that was needed was more people. And the reason Llanwern was a mess was another illustration of the difficulties governments get themselves into when they are tempted to put a large political component into industrial issues.

In the run-up to the 1959 general election a decision had to be made about investment in a new hot strip mill and associ-ated steelmaking plant for that part of the industry which had not been denationalised after 1951. The Prime Minister, Harold Macmillan, saw at once that a substantial project of this kind could only redound to the credit of his administration and, therefore, if one strip mill was good, two would be even better.

The investment was consequently divided between Ravenscraig, at Motherwell in Scotland, and Llanwern. This meant, to put it briefly, that Llanwern could not make enough steel to satisfy the capacity of its rolling mills, a bad enough outcome in itself from a production point of view but one which, because of the structure of pay and bonus rates, was instrumental in making the works a by-word for appalling industrial relations.

But Llanwern was also supposed to represent the future. Its capacity, in theory, anyway, was three times that of the steel-making plant at Ebbw Vale, and its position on the coast essential for a large-scale operation which relied on the import by sea of iron ore. It was, like Port Talbot, just the sort of place that would figure largely in the BSC's plan for a huge expansion of steel production in Britain, based on perhaps five such deep water sites. You only had to look at what the Japanese were doing to see that it didn't just make sense, it was the only route to survival. Of course it didn't work.

An essential part of this plan was the closure of the small steelworks, although not necessarily of some of their associated production like tinplate, of which South Wales was the sole British producer, and the loss of large numbers of jobs. In Wales alone steelmaking had to end not only at Ebbw Vale, but at Shotton and at East Moors in Cardiff. The steel corporation had these in their sights all along, probably from the first day of its existence, but the scale of the problem they presented made everyone pause.

Even though, as I've said, Lord Melchett had been to Ebbw Vale in the spring of 1969 to reveal his plans, there was a sense that perhaps the whole nasty business might go away. Perhaps, somehow, he didn't mean it. People like John Powell didn't think so, but that was no reason not to keep trying, in particular to introduce as much delay as possible. It was at least a method of buying time while finding other ways of meeting the problems with which the area would be confronted. The result was that it wasn't until something like five years after nationalisation that we were introduced to the institution that became known as Monty Finniston's Flying Circus.

This was the name given to the line of Rovers and Jaguars that toured the steelworks of Wales to deliver the black spot. It was named after Dr (later Sir) Monty Finniston, an excitable, high-pitched man from the Glasgow working classes, who was the corporation's Chief Executive and who became, after Melchett's death, its Chairman. He was the man with the big plan and he frequently found himself unable to contain his frustration at the fact that while the British steel industry decayed and fell further and further behind the rest of the world, nothing was bloody well happening. "I'll give you the answer to that in one word. Balls," he told me on one occasion, in answer to my question about some supposed difficulty in the way of his hugely ambitious expansionist scheme.

Making some efforts to push on, in November 1972 Melchett was in Ebbw Vale, this time announcing the real figures – at least four and a half thousand jobs to go. In December he was in Cardiff, offering the last rites to East Moors. The next month he was in Shotton with more of the same. It was there he crossed the room to speak to me and murmur a bleak joke. "We can't go on meeting like this," he said.

However, that still wasn't the end of the matter. On taking office on March 1974, the Labour Government decided the whole strategy had to be examined all over again. An industry minister, Lord Beswick, was sent to tour the country, looking at the cases being made over the threatened steelworks. Another year went by while Lord Beswick did his sums. After something like another year he put forward an amended scheme, which meant changes and delays, although it did accept the closure of steelmaking at Ebbw Vale. Even then Lord Beswick's investigation was by no means complete.

Anyone who went to those places and saw the passion with which people defended their jobs and understood what this closure programme meant couldn't fail to sympathise with their arguments. But there was another problem that couldn't be ignored for much longer. Years after the industry was nationalised it wasn't producing an ounce more steel than it had been in the first place while, ominously, productivity levels in Japan and Germany were four times those in Britain. In 1968, Port Talbot, a works marked out as having an important role in the new strategy, employed more than seventeen thousand men when the figure should have been perhaps four thousand. No wonder the works was known as Treasure Island and the town was the first in Wales to have a casino. It really couldn't go on like this, although it did do so for rather longer than anyone might have anticipated.

In the steel corporation's headquarters at Grosvenor Place in London, Monty Finniston boiled away with impatience at obstacles that constantly sprang up in his path. He thought he knew what had to be done but he wasn't allowed to do it. He thought if he didn't do it then the industry in Britain would either be effectively wiped out or limp along indefinitely, consuming increasing amounts of Government subsidy. In a risky move he explained that dilemma in some detail at a dinner he held for journalists. He told us what had to close, how many jobs had to go even, or perhaps especially, in the works that would remain. In industrial terms it was apocalyptic: sixty thousand redundancies.

It was all the more shocking because while industrialists might have thought such things they never, ever, uttered them in public. That was emphatically the case when they were, in effect, employed by a Labour government. It was so dangerous, so reckless that I had to ask: did he really mean we could use this stuff? Definitely. Did it make any difference? Not the one Finniston intended: a year or so later the Government decided not to renew Sir Monty's contract and he abruptly ceased to be Chairman of the British Steel Corporation.

People argue now that Finniston's scheme was impossibly ambitious, that he could never have built the huge steel industry he was planning for the country. Despite that, though, he did have some kind of vision whereas most people, in government, in industry, in the unions, didn't really grasp what was going on in old industrial Britain, in places like Wales. They saw a series of events but not a consistent pattern. Or if they discerned the pattern they were overwhelmed by the vast problems with which it confronted them.

The journalist Geoffrey Goodman, for a long time industrial editor of the *Daily Mirror*, was an adviser to the Wilson Government for a period in the sixties. "We were talking about half the workforce having to be dismissed in order to make those plants cost-effective and people weren't prepared to do it.

Even the management, even the toughest, most ruthless management, when they saw the implications of what they'd need to do in order to compete with the Japanese or the Germans, when they saw the implications of the numbers of people who had to be sacked, they shrivelled and shrank from it. It was understandable because there was no social plan. You could argue that there never has been a social plan to cope with the dimensions of the problem. They backed off because they already had the first glimmerings of the magnitude of the social problem. They knew that, given modern technology, hundreds of thousands of workers in steel, in shipbuilding, in mining, in construction, in heavy engineering and the rest would have to be laid off, but they really didn't know how to tackle it. The truth of the matter is that the problem was so big and the implications of the problem were so big that there was never any overall agreement. They never got round the Cabinet table and said: 'This is how we're going to tackle it. This is our plan.' They didn't have a plan."

Of course the Heath Government hadn't had a plan either. Or they'd started with one but changed it as they went along. But those years between 1970 and 1974 played as significant a part as any in misleading people about the true nature of the changes looming over a huge section of British society. Nowadays it's an article of faith that 'the miners were shafted by Thatcher', and while no-one imagines she was in any way distressed by the ultimate humiliation of Arthur Scargill, she could not have done it alone. She needed the unwitting co-operation of Scargill himself but the origins of what is now presented as a bitter defeat for the National Union of Mineworkers in fact lay in the heady days of the union's greatest industrial triumphs.

It's difficult today to capture the persistent atmosphere of conflict that, even fewer than twenty years ago, characterised much of industrial life in Britain. A substantial part of my working day might often be spent looking for those locations where we could get some strife-torn works in the background while I recited to camera the details of the latest industrial relations disaster. The motor industry with its proliferation of trades unions was a laughing stock. Half a dozen people walking out at the component manufacturers Lucas could bring car production lines all over Britain to a standstill. Strikes in the steel industry at times sometimes took on the character of some kind of obscure sporting contest in which the actual dispute served only to get the game started, like the kick-off at football.

I spent much of the summer of 1969 in Port Talbot, for example, where steel production was stopped as the blast-furnacemen struck over the issue of an extra pound a week to which they might, or might not, have been entitled. Eventually, as other British industries were threatened by a lack of steel supplies, a way had to be found of giving it to them. At the court of inquiry set up by the Government to resolve the question or, more accurately, provide a quick fix, it emerged that their real grievances concerned other matters entirely. At Llanwern, where large numbers of employees bothered turning up for work only now and again, although a system of organised dishonesty meant they were officially on the premises and so paid, industrial relations were so dreadful that eventually even the unions were embarrassed and joined the management in an inquiry into the problems there.

It often seemed unlikely that any large-scale civil engineering project would get finished at all as a strike might well be called over whose turn it was to make the tea. A full-time official of a small construction union used to ring me regularly to report on some walk-out or other. "The boys are very worried," he might say, "about the situation in Vietnam and they've stopped work in protest." This was a way of conducting industrial life that was so familiar then it scarcely raised an eyebrow. It took the National Union of Mineworkers to create the new mythology of industrial action.

What happened during the two miners' strikes of the early seventies was so remarkable that for a long time it persuaded people that the world really had changed. The NUM and its predecessor organisations hadn't staged an official national strike since the bitter days of 1926 and there was no particular reason to think that it would ever do so again. It was a declining industry and, whenever there was unrest over pay settlements, the National Coal Board would warn that more money would mean more pit closures and fewer jobs. But that was happening anyway. Fifty thousand mining jobs disappeared from South

Wales between 1959 and 1969 and eventually people began to question what the benefits were of being complaisant. Towards the end of the sixties attitudes began to change in the industry, and South Wales was one of the areas where an unofficial left-wing movement emerged to drive the union towards a new militancy.

It led eventually to one of the most tumultuous periods of industrial action ever seen in Britain, certainly one of the most significant. In 1972 the miners humiliated a government. Two years later they drove it out of office and moved from heroic mortality into mythology. The union and its members could do anything. On the Monday of one miners' annual conference in Porthcawl, the South Wales President, Emlyn Williams, attacked the government. The stock market fell sharply. The next morning as he strolled along the front he said cheerfully: "I've made some investments so today I'm going to say nice things about the government. Push prices back up again." It was one of those jokes which carried within it almost as much as you would need to know about the NUM's view of who really ran Britain. It also, revealingly, carried more than an element of the truth. Even as late as February 1981, Mrs Thatcher personally intervened to head off the threat of industrial action against a planned pit closure programme. The miners could lick all-comers.

The NUM's achievements during that period were quite remarkable and often applauded by a wider public which believed that men willing to face the grim conditions and physical hazards of being miners should be properly rewarded. They had a grip on people's emotions which no other occupation has ever shared. They had the solidarity of their own communities, the sympathy of those outside who could not imagine how much they would need to be paid to work underground and the support of the mining diaspora, the descendants of so many people who had trailed away from the coalfields between the wars, looking for work. For a time they represented an idealised, almost romantic, image of the British working man as hero.

But their celebrated triumphs also led many people to come to some dangerously wrong conclusions. One was that nationalised industries were not subject to the same constraints as the private sector. When the Coal Board, faced with a pay demand, said it didn't have any money, that was not treated as a serious argument. The government had money, all they had to do was to hand it over. And, sure enough, when circumstances were difficult enough, the government did hand it over. The lesson was not wasted on other trades unions.

The second consequence was to elevate the reputation of industrial action as a method of negotiation, especially in the public sector. If the miners, who'd been pushed around for years, could do it, so could others. The problem was understood clearly enough by George Wright who came to Wales in the early seventies as regional secretary of the Transport and General Workers Union and who was instrumental in setting up the Wales TUC, of which he became the first general secretary.

"In my view unions in the 1970s were inebriated with the power that had generated from the settlement of the miners' strike. Indeed, it was not unknown for me to have to intervene in a dispute where the workers were asking for more at the end than they had at the beginning of the dispute. In this they were following the example set by the miners in 1972 who, when the Wilberforce Report awarded them all they'd gone on strike for, refused to settle and forced the Government into conceding even more."

The culture of dispute was ingrained in the seventies at least in part, George Wright believes, because of a failure of leadership in many of the unions, a willingness of officials to be pushed into action by their members. The culmination of it all was what became known as the Winter of Discontent, that eruption of strikes, particularly within the public services, which disfigured the winter of 1978-79. "It was then and only then," Wright argues, "with the defeat of that dispute and the loss of the Labour Government that people within the unions began to recognise that the time had come for change. It was, of course, altogether too late. The damage had been done."

The consequence was far more than the loss of a single election. These events coloured the public view of the unions and, by extension the Labour Party, for a whole political generation. The idea of something called the Labour movement, a partnership between the unions and the party, was changed for ever by what happened in those years, although it took much longer for that to be grasped by most of the participants. Jim Callaghan clearly sensed it on the day he left Downing Street in May 1979, defeated by his own side as much as anything. Geoffrey Goodman talked to him on that day. "He said something to me which I've never forgotten. He said: 'Well, we've lost, but maybe we needed to lose. Maybe the country needs somebody like Margaret Thatcher to kick it into shape.'"

Despite such grim insights, however, the penny still didn't drop for some people. In January 1980 the Iron and Steel Trades Confederation, the main union in the steel industry, went on strike in support of a pay claim. The dispute lasted for more than three months and ended with the steel corporation increasing its offer from two per cent to six per cent (or sixteen per cent, depending on how you like to do the calculations). It was only then that the union realised it had been on strike over the wrong issue. It was talking about pay when it should have been thinking about jobs. It was a rude awakening.

George Wright blames everyone involved, including the unions, for this air of fantasy, the idea that the rules of economics, of profit and loss, were somehow indefinitely suspended as far as they were concerned. "I think the British Steel management had become so accustomed to carrying the begging bowl to Parliament that they failed to manage the industry sensibly. In fact I was appalled at the practices which continued to exist; the unwillingness of workers to face up to change, the constant belief that someone would always save you; the idea that if you had a problem in a steelworks in Wales you could buy a rail ticket to London and someone would find the answer for you. It was almost impossible to get them to change direction – the workers in their plants, the unions who led them but, above all, those who managed them."

A measure of the unreality of the situation was that, when Mrs Thatcher took office, the British Steel Corporation was losing a million pounds *a day*. The evil moment could be postponed no longer. If it was to survive at all then there had to be redundancies on a scale that would have been previously unimaginable. All the things that hadn't been done would now be accomplished with calamitous speed. It wasn't just in steel, although that was where the axe fell most obviously in Wales. We were in fact launched on a process of rapid de-industrialisation which involved wholesale social change. It marked the end of Wales as most people had understood it, as indeed it marked a similar transformation for many other parts of industrial Britain. It was a brutal experience, all the more so because it had been so long delayed. It raised the question of what might have happened if governments, employers and unions had had more vision, more foresight, more determination to make changes when they could have been more humanely managed.

This is important because it hasn't been simply a question of watching the unemployment figures rocket as old industries closed and then subside somewhat as other occupations filled some of the gaps created. Just as important was the way in which people saw themselves, which is why the men of Ebbw Vale talked contemptuously about the new work that might be available in the marshmallow factory or making dolls' eyes. Here the word "men" is important: it was men who worked underground, in the steel mills, the blast furnaces, the docks. The social order that implied, in particular the relationships between the sexes, had seemed immutable. People could now feel the ground shifting under their feet and perhaps it's not too far fetched to look at that outburst of industrial disorder in the seventies at least in part as a last despairing effort to hold on to a familiar way of life.

During the 1983 election campaign I put to Mrs Thatcher a view which had been voiced by a Labour MP. Although the figures of people without jobs were going almost vertically up the graph she actually saw unemployment as the solution rather than as the problem. She paused for an interval that could only have been detected by the most sensitive measuring equipment before ignoring the question and going to say what she had always intended to say. But that moment's hesitation revealed a great deal. She knew there was an important sense in which this accusation was true and in which it was to become even more significant. Industrial relations legislation might have played its part in shifting relationships between employers and workers, particularly in the public sector, but it was clear that it was the sword of unemployment rather than that of justice which made the difference as people confronted the harsh truths of a new economic and social order.

It's been an inexorable process. Tiger Bay, once a legend around the world for its colour, its vibrancy and its danger, is now Cardiff Bay, Europe's most exciting waterfront development as it's called, in a world where the word development can be as much a threat as a promise and the word exciting the last refuge of an uninspired advertising agency. From their penthouse flats armchair sailors can look at the television producers, designers, solicitors, civil servants and restaurant owners as they go about their business among the still waters of what was once one of the world's busiest ports. It couldn't have been left as it was simply to decline and decay, but one of the reasons the project was so vehemently opposed by some people must surely have been an awareness of the break with the past it represented. The certainties of one kind of society, however resented they might have been, were being replaced with a prefabricated future, erected almost overnight.

Perhaps if that day in Ebbw Vale in February 1975 represented one landmark in this process, another, just as significant, was the day ten years later when the miners, after eleven months on strike, went back to work without a settlement between them and the National Coal Board. It was the last spasm of that brief period in their history when the NUM seemed to represent not only the aspirations, but the potential, of British working people. It not only marked, as Arthur Scargill correctly said it would, the last days of most of Britain's coal mining industry, but of the legend of the miners. Scargill has to take much of the blame for this although the Coal Board chairman, Ian McGregor, a man who once put a plastic bag over his head to pretend he wasn't there, made a substantial contribution to the intractability of the dispute. Mrs Thatcher, with a majority of 144, welcomed the chance to confront and defeat the NUM. The Government had prepared for it and, while it claimed to be above the battle, was actually exerting constant pressure on the strategies being employed to fight it.

In these circumstances it was a curious thing that Scargill, assumed by most people to be a capable strategist, should have fallen into such a huge error of judgement and to have persisted in it for so long. He did so against the better understanding of people like the miners' leaders in South Wales and he split his own union in the process. The accepted explanation is that Scargill was a victim of his own propaganda, his belief that nothing could stand in the way of the organised determination of the British miner. "The miners, united, will never be defeated," they would chant, only in the end to prove the reverse – the miners, defeated, will never be united, and they have not been since. This was not an industrial relations dispute on however large a scale, but a trial of strength in which Scargill in particular was a prisoner of his own history. That history, and much that went with it, was now at an end.

The Long Journey

It was twenty-five past four in the morning of Friday, September 19 1997, and it really was time to go home.

Anyone with an IQ in double figures could see that the Welsh public (or that proportion of them that could be bothered to vote) had delivered a clear judgement on the idea of an elected Welsh assembly. Thanks, but no thanks, was their answer although they had perhaps put the rejection rather more politely than they had the last time they were asked. The referee might not have blown the final whistle but we were in extra time, the result was clear and the crowd, as it does at rugby matches, was starting to drift away.

In Studio 6, the BBC's main current affairs radio studio in Cardiff, only Lord Elis-Thomas – the former Plaid Cymru MP Dafydd Elis Thomas – was unwilling to concede that it was all over but to the rest of us his attitude seemed to be taking optimism to the point of psychiatric disorder. There was only one referendum result to come and the 'Yes' camp were sixteen thousand votes behind the 'Noes'. None of the twenty-one results we had already heard suggested that this deficit was likely to be overturned by the voters of Carmarthen, whose judgement we were awaiting.

Some time before, admittedly, something stronger than a rumour had emerged, suggesting that this final result would provide a sensational twist. The system adopted for declaring the results had meant that, all night, well-founded forecasts had been emerging long before the official figures were announced. But even as I broadcast this speculation it was impossible to believe it could really happen. Soon we could say goodbye to the few listeners still up and hurry along the corridor where there might possibly still be a glass of free BBC wine and a curly sandwich to restore us after five and a half hours continuous broadcasting.

At last a man called Brad Roynon, the chief executive of Carmarthenshire County Council, made his way to the microphone. With great punctiliousness he began to read the result in

Welsh, a language he was apparently seeing for the first time that morning. In Studio 6 and elsewhere people, Welsh and English speakers alike, strained to make sense of his halting syllables. It might just as well have been Hungarian. Then... could he really have said...? Yes, he had. Carmarthenshire had voted in favour, and had done so by a majority of almost twenty-three thousand. The 'Yes' camp's wake at the *Park Hotel* in Cardiff turned, in an instant, into a party. Some campaigners wept openly in front of the cameras as others danced and clapped and sang and cheered. Everywhere there was a sense of disbelief.

It is impossible to think of a more extraordinary event in modern British political life, such a thunderously theatrical climax to what had been a pedestrian and uninspiring drama – the devolution campaign itself during which large parts of the audience either fell asleep or took the opportunity to leave the auditorium early. More than a million people had voted and more than a million hadn't bothered. By a majority almost impossible to discern with the naked eye, they had changed the nature of Welsh politics, and perhaps British politics too.

Eighteen years earlier, on March 2, 1979, I had sat in another studio, downstairs in Broadcasting House, Cardiff, telling Welsh viewers a different story about another referendum. In that event it needed only the first result to indicate as clearly as was possible that plans for an elected Welsh assembly had been decisively, even contemptuously, rejected by the Welsh public. If Gwynedd wasn't going to buy it you could be certain no-one else would. How, I wondered all those years later, had we got from there to here?

It was very much in keeping with the melodramatic nature of the events of September 1997 that, three days after the referendum, George Thomas, Viscount Tonypandy, breathed his last. I'm not suggesting that the news had proved too much for the sick and frail old man, but his death further underlined the sense of change of those days, particularly in the light of his obsessive opposition to anything that smacked of Welsh nationalism. Sometimes, in his partisan prime, when he uttered the word "nationalist" you could hear the sizzle of his contempt.

The job of Speaker of the House of Commons, in which

George (as he was invariably known to those who knew him, and those who didn't) rose to international fame, demands in particular that the occupant of the Chair should put party behind him and deal with people and events with a judicious even-handedness. Who but George in this exalted position would have gloated so much over the Government's four-to-one defeat in the 1979 devolution referendum in Wales that he felt he had to ring his old colleague, the former Secretary of State for Wales Cledwyn Hughes, to, as he put it, "express his delight"?

"He [Cledwyn Hughes] angrily retorted that I was supposed to be neutral. It gave me enormous pleasure to say, 'Oh yes. As Speaker I am entirely impartial, but on this issue I know on whose side I am impartial!'" As I read those words again I can hear the malicious relish in his voice as he indulged one of his favourite hobbies: paying off old scores. And who but George would have put this anecdote into his memoirs as apparently reflecting credit on him?

George invariably went about his daily business with an unquenchable, Christian effusiveness. He could not see a hand without shaking it, he exuded so much sincerity and goodwill to all men you could have bottled it and sold it to the United Nations. This kind of behaviour was so compulsive that people outside politics assumed that it was all there was to it, that he was a bit of a mild holy roller without an ounce of malice in him. The truth was rather different because he was also as combative and ruthless a politician as you could meet in a very long walk through Westminster, a man fuelled by an explosive mixture of vanity and ambition. He had a long memory for any slight, real or imagined, and was a particularly dangerous enemy. He was also very funny, with a sharp, rather camp humour, which made him a successful Speaker in very difficult parliamentary times. But for all his experience, determination and skill he turned out to lack the one talent essential for a really successful politician: judgement.

It's easy enough to sit around thirty years and more after the events and discern the patterns in political life which have led us to our present position. It was not so simple in the sixties and the seventies and the eighties, I can testify, but the strand of

Labour politics George Thomas often tactlessly represented was increasingly out of tune with the times.

This failing was exacerbated by a characteristic which many of us, particularly journalists, find attractive in politicians: his inclination to denounce in the most scathing manner anything of which he disapproved. When it came to political argument he took no prisoners. On one occasion during a frustrating debate in the Commons he turned on Raymond Gower, the Conservative MP for Barry, a genial man who wasn't much interested in questions of party. (Asked a question about South Africa during an election campaign Gower once said: "If I'd known this was going to be political I wouldn't have agreed to come.") George looked at him across the chamber and pronounced: "The Honourable Member is the biggest traitor Barry has had since Judas Iscariot." Who had realised, until that moment, that Judas was a Barry boy?

At another time he said of the Conservative Secretary of State, Peter Thomas, a gentle man of immense charm and goodwill, someone who would leave out of his speeches the partisan jibes that others had painstakingly written in: "The Secretary of State needn't worry about being bothered by people in the streets of Cardiff. They wouldn't recognise him, apart from the trail of slime he leaves as he makes his way from the station to the Welsh Office." It's no wonder that the young Nicholas Edwards, watching from the Government benches, was to say he learnt a great deal about technique from watching George, which no doubt explains why Edwards became one of the most abrasive (not to mention loudest) debaters in Welsh political life in the last thirty years. From where I sat, though, he didn't appear to be much in need of a role model to perfect this talent.

While George's performances brought some much-needed entertainment to the conduct of Welsh politics at Westminster, which has always been able to do with all the cheering-up it can get, it became increasingly clear that there was a need for someone with more imagination and a more conciliatory cast of mind to be the Labour Party's leading figure in Wales. His fierce hatred of nationalism spilled over into an ill-concealed impatience with Welsh language activists. It was often clear that to him the language was not just an irrelevance, but, more danger-ously, nationalist politics in fancy dress.

"Seen these latest figures on the Welsh language, George?" I asked at a party conference when he was Shadow Secretary of State. The numbers of Welsh speakers had fallen yet again. "Couldn't sleep a wink all night for thinking about them," he said, and wheezed with laughter at his own joke.

Well, he had to go, didn't he? Politics in Wales were changing and leaving George behind. So, to everyone's surprise, most of all George's, his pal Harold Wilson didn't reappoint him as Welsh Secretary when Labour crept back into office in the election of February 1974. The place he had expected to resume in the Cabinet went instead to John Morris, the MP for Aberavon, a Welsh-speaking, pro-devolution lawyer, culturally someone who was about as far from George as you could get and still be in the same party.

Some years later, sitting, very pleased with himself once more, in the Speaker's House in Westminster, George told me: "I was bitterly disappointed when I didn't become Secretary of State again. Bitterly disappointed. Still, as I said to Harold: 'One door closes and another opens. No doubt John Morris has got talents I haven't got.'" Then, as ever, he couldn't resist adding, with a tap on my knee: "Mind you, I wonder what they were, having seen him in action."

The assassination of George had the fingerprints of an even tougher politician all over it. As someone who'd been MP for a neighbouring Cardiff constituency for almost thirty years, Jim Callaghan, second in seniority only to the Prime Minister, knew the dangers of a nat-bashing Secretary of State at this stage. And Callaghan was certainly urged on by other senior figures in the Labour Party in Wales, some of whom George regarded as little more than nationalist fellow-travellers.

In fact there were three strands of opinion in the Labour Party at that time. Those who thought that, whatever the circumstances, a measure of devolution was in itself a good idea. Then there were those who wanted to find some way of dish-ing the nationalists and weren't too choosy about the methods used. And finally there were those who thought devolution was a bad idea for a number of reasons, chiefly because they believed it would undermine the authority of the United Kingdom Parliament and its ability to act in the interests of places like Wales. They later added to their arguments the view that even if devolution were good in principle, the scheme put forward by the Government was a dreadful way of implementing it – in short, a dog's breakfast. The fact that such diverse views were contained in the Labour Party alone were a recipe for disaster, which in due course arrived.

It seemed to me at the time that the central problem with the Government's devolution plans was that they were firmly rooted in the age-old political principle of what's the least we can get away with? Things like secondary legislation, which I won't explain now and of which hardly anyone had ever heard, were suddenly revealed to have stupendous constitutional importance. On the other hand the proposed Welsh assembly wouldn't be able to make laws or raise money, without which powers an organisation of any kind is severely constrained in finding useful things to do. You don't have to have a research degree in constitutional studies to realise quite quickly that this is pretty much the same sort of scheme as was proposed and endorsed in 1997. In these circumstances a compelling question is why people's attitudes, or enough people's attitudes anyway, changed over eighteen and a half years towards what was, in essence, the same proposal.

I believe one reason is that, in the vote of 1979, and in the years of argument and parliamentary debate that led up to it, many people took a cynical view of the way in which politicians went round embracing as matters of profound philosophical conviction theories and actions which were clearly chiefly designed to keep them in office. Not all of them were like that, but enough to keep the voters on their sceptical toes. "There's nothing as powerful as an idea whose time has come," Callaghan said of devolution in Swansea in 1979, in one of those effortlessly meaningless slogans for which a politician can never be called to account. His true level of enthusiasm can be gauged from the fact that when, many years later, I mentioned the matter of devolution in passing, he said briskly: "I inherited that," and changed the subject.

The truth was that devolution was an increasingly desperate

search for a way out of a pressing political difficulty, but one which might well have been over-estimated. It began with Gwynfor Evans's victory in the Carmarthen by-election in July 1966, the first time Plaid Cymru had ever won a parliamentary seat. Winnie Ewing won Hamilton for the SNP the following year. In 1967 Plaid Cymru ran Labour close in a by-election in Rhondda West and closer still in Caerphilly the year after that. Welsh language activists were lying in the roads and tearing down signs. A certain amount of light terrorism was going on. Even with a majority of nearly a hundred, the Labour Government started casting round for things to do about it.

It found two. One was to organise the Investiture of the Prince of Wales in Caernarfon Castle in July 1969, following the example set in 1911 by Lloyd George, far and away the most brilliant politician in modern Welsh history. In *The People's Champion*, the second volume of his biography of Lloyd George, John Grigg says of the plan to invent some ceremony for the Investiture of the future Edward VIII: "He saw it would enable him to gratify Welsh national pride and, at the same time, to reassure traditionalists in every part of the Kingdom."

The very thing, Harold Wilson must have said to himself, and everyone had a good time, in particular the Queen's then brother-in-law, the Earl of Snowdon, who pranced around the castle in a natty uniform he invented for himself. It's difficult to say how much such things "reassured traditionalists" but, as it turned out in later years, the Royal Family might have been well advised to consider the rather unfortunate example set by the subsequent career of the first man to be put through this bogus ceremony. I somehow doubt if there'll be another.

The other stratagem was equally traditional and equally devious. In April 1969 the Government set up a royal commission to look into the constitution, thus allowing any questions about the matter to be safely deferred in the years and years such bodies take to trundle around the country not coming up with the answers. In the perspective of politics a week is a long time and a royal commission is the equivalent of several thousand light years. It goes straight into the drawer marked "Oblivion".

And, indeed, by the time the commission reported in November 1973, Labour had been out of power for more than three years. A Conservative Government, led by Edward Heath or anyone else, wasn't in the business of messing around with the constitution, so no-one needed to bother spending too much time studying the conclusions of the Kilbrandon (né Crowther) Commission in all their perplexing richness and variety. Heath said the report should have "a proper consideration", which is what in Downing Street they call the waste-paper basket. As it thudded on to our desks, however, the lights were going out and we began to enjoy the rigours of the three-day week.

A couple of months after that Heath was asking the British public who they thought ought to be running the country – him or the National Union of Mineworkers. Not you, anyway, was the voters' dusty response, and we were unexpectedly launched on the most tumultuous period of political activity that Britain had seen since the War. At the centre of it was the critical question of how the economy should be run, but the parliamentary arithmetic meant that, in order to do anything at all, even to give the appearance of actually running the country, the Government had to keep on board not only the nationalists but the Liberals, to whom all constitutional issues are, if not the red meat of politics, at least the nut cutlet.

The February election of 1974 put two members of Plaid Cymru, Dafydd Wigley and Dafydd Elis Thomas, into the Commons – the first time Plaid Cymru had won seats at a general election. Gwynfor Evans failed to regain Carmarthen by three votes, a deficit the voters, particularly anti-Labour voters, were keen to remedy the following October. Eleven members of the Scottish Nationalist Party were also elected. Wilson had no overall majority in the first election of 1974 and only the scraps of one in the second. It was a time for flexibility.

"We were spoilt, really, from day one," Dafydd Elis Thomas recalled later. "Wigley and I were embraced by the Welsh Labour Party, which is the worst thing that could happen to any Welsh politician both within and outside that party, I think. The first time I ever went to the House of Lords was to have a glass of dry sherry at lunchtime with Lord Crowther-Hunt who was then responsible for devolution in the Wilson Government.

"I used to get phone calls every Sunday from the Government's Deputy Chief Whip, Walter Harrison, to check what the Plaid Cymru parliamentary group had decided on any particular vote. I was obviously seen as the sort of soft touch of the group as far as Labour were concerned then. I tried to use my position to influence the party position in Wales and also to influence the Labour Government."

The Government knew it had to do something, but wasn't very clear on what it might be. It was perhaps significant that they brought in Norman Hunt, an Oxford don, as a constitutional adviser and later, as Dafydd Elis Thomas's sherry-drinking companion Lord Crowther-Hunt, a minister. Hunt had been on the Kilbrandon Commission whose only coherent conclusion was that there should be some change in the constitution without there being any serious consensus on what that change might be. The members between them offered a bewildering series of options for Scotland and Wales; Hunt and a colleague added to them by writing a substantial memorandum of dissent which included plans for devolution to the English regions as well. This was no way, as they say, to run a railroad.

In these circumstances any proposal was bound to look like some disreputable political fix, but even that might not have mattered if the Government had been able to carry its own supporters with it. Instead, for two years from December 1976 until November 1978, as the Government wrestled its devolution legislation through Parliament, it was constantly at odds with the some of the most able and articulate members on its own side. Timetables were wrecked, referendums were introduced then referendum thresholds inserted, the legislation chipped away at. Night after night a few of us sat up in the press gallery wondering if the Government was going to muster a majority for this clause or that. Quite often it didn't. It was politics at its most gripping and another illustration of the fact that the best political arguments are often within parties rather than between them. And, as if that weren't enough, they were at the same time smashing each other to bits over the economy.

Six Welsh Labour MPs openly denounced the legislation and there were others who, although enjoined to silence because they were ministers, were known to be opposed. Neil Kinnock was as noisy and passionate and fluent and adjectival as ever ("What's he going to do when something really important comes up?" people would ask, as Westminster rang to his rhetoric). But for my money Leo Abse, one of the most gifted backbenchers of his time as a manipulator of Parliament ("You love Parliament, I use it," he once told Michael Foot) was the one who really touched the nerve of the Welsh public. A Welsh assembly, his argument ran, would be a gravy train for the kind of people we had all seen running local councils, people whose wish was not to serve their constituents but to help themselves to the contents of the local authority cash register.

Such people had legendary status, particularly in industrial South Wales. Some had recently gone to gaol. When, for example, the Queen reached Swansea on her Jubilee tour and opened the city's new leisure centre, the loyal cheers that greeted her could no doubt be heard clearly by one of those principally responsible for the project as he sat in his cell in the nearby prison.

Job-seekers carried bottles of Scotch to influential councillors; funny handshakes were exchanged; a nephew's name would be written in a small notebook; planning permission became a form of currency; a nice day out in London and perhaps a coat for the wife were the small change of building contracts; the stern admonition on job advertisements, "Canvassing will disqualify", was a form of ironic humour.

I feel certain, though, that some of the mighty figures who ruled their county councils with such a grip never took a dishonest penny in their lives. They were men who loved the exercise of power for its own sake. They would decide who got what job, who sat where, who had a parking space and who didn't. Perhaps the greatest of them all was Llew Heycock, later Lord Heycock of Taibach, a man, I am sure, of the utmost financial rectitude and, because he's dead, I don't *have* to say that. On one occasion in Canada, where most people had never heard of Taibach, or Port Talbot, or even Glamorgan County Council, he was mystified when he was not given a place in the front row to watch a rugby match. He turned to his wife and said: "They are treating us like ordinary people," an experience neither of them had undergone for decades.

In these circumstances it wasn't difficult for Abse to make people's flesh creep with his warnings of corruption, a message that might have been rather less uncritically received from Westminster twenty years later, a time when MPs with their hands out and trousers down pranced daily through the pages of the national newspapers. It's clear enough that all the crooks and despots haven't been driven out of local government in Wales during the last couple of decades, or out of other areas of public life come to that, but somehow the issue didn't have the same bite by 1997. In 1979, though, it was to be one illustration of how the argument over devolution became an argument about the state of Wales itself.

In the same way an outburst from Neil Kinnock in the Commons one night stripped the thin skin from another of the controversies the devolution debate wasn't supposed to be about. Quite what constitutional point was involved is now entirely forgotten, but what he had to say went to the heart of unspoken resentments. In some schools on Anglesey, he told MPs at full Kinnockian volume, children were not allowed to go to the lavatory unless they asked in Welsh to do so. Many people took the implication to be that, under a Welsh assembly, there'd be a lot more of that kind of thing as it sent its jack-booted language police goose-stepping through the education system and anywhere else they could break down the doors.

Kinnock didn't mean anything of the kind of course, but political debate isn't a particularly rational process and it was a contribution which inflamed the argument, encouraged by Welsh Tories in particular, that one of the consequences of devolution would be the imposition of a particular linguistic agenda by the cultural commissars of the North. This is an entirely laughable idea to anyone who's spent even ten minutes with the average South Wales Labour politician, someone who, when it comes to exercising control, makes the late Joe Stalin look like John Major.

But that is to miss the point. Eventually the debate itself became the important issue, rather than what the debate was about. So it was possible to tell people in South Wales that people from the North would soon be marching down to force feed them phonetic mutations, while at the same time those in the North could be warned that they'd never get public money for industrial development because no cash would be allowed any nearer them than Merthyr Tydfil. All this was another reminder that politics is often little more than institutionalised prejudice.

Nevertheless, it also raises the significant issue of the impact of the language on Welsh political life. For example, if the energy, ingenuity and dedication that has been put into Welsh language campaigns since the early nineteen-sixties had been focused instead on something more broadly recognisable as Welsh politics, would Wales now look a lot more like Scotland? Maybe, without the language, the people involved would just have stayed in bed, or joined the Militant Tendency, but the particular political vigour and enterprise of that generation was channelled towards essentially narrow ends, however worthy, and however much the people involved saw them as central to their idea of what Wales was. It was often brilliantly done through a judicious mixture of blackmail and the begging-bowl, but this kind of single-issue politics presents a problem in the wider world if the merits of a policy have to be decided, at least in part, by its impact on a minority language, especially when eighty per cent of the population don't speak that language.

At one and the same time the language has been both instrumental in there being Welsh politics at all and an obstacle to its progress. It has, for example, given Plaid Cymru a philosophical respectability but has persistently made the party seem alien to the majority. I know there are lots of people in Plaid Cymru who don't speak Welsh but, despite that, the language has an important role in defining what the party is. I have never, for example, heard anyone make a speech in Welsh at a Labour Party conference, while in Plaid Cymru it's always been considered important to use the language if you can and, sometimes, even if you can't.

That's one of the reasons why, despite some sporadically interesting results in various elections in industrial Wales, the party's strength, particularly in parliamentary terms, remains in the Welsh-speaking rural areas and is unable to haul itself much above ten per cent of the popular vote. The Scottish National Party doesn't have a matching problem, although if you like principle in your politics it's worth remembering that the SNP's impetus in the seventies came substantially from greed, as voters were urged to think about the prospect of getting their hands on all that North Sea oil: rich Scotland and poor England, as the slogan of the time had it.

It seems to me that in Wales the language for many years skewed the argument because of its prominence in political debate and the ease with which governments, Labour and Conservative, have been able and willing to respond to what are, by UK standards, modest demands. Bilingual forms, a Welsh Language Act, some money for the National Eisteddfod, a television channel, another Welsh Language Act – here you are, now go away and don't bother me again until next time. It's the politics of the rich uncle, but it has been divisive within Wales because it has been presented as a way in which a small minority, almost some kind of secret society, has sought undue privilege and influence. The truth or otherwise of this view is neither here nor there: what people think to be the case is as important as what actually is the case.

I get the distinct impression, though, that this matters less in the nineties than it did in the seventies. Some of the arguments have been defused, especially that over broadcasting which was perhaps the most provocative issue both for those who spoke Welsh and those who didn't. This has had the effect of making the language less of an intrusion into the daily lives of people who prefer to live in monoglot English heaven and, in the nature of things, the more television there is, the less it all seems to matter. Not all disputes have been downgraded; there will always be explosions over education, for example, but it does seem that a reasonable accommodation has now been reached by the various participants in most of the linguistic arguments.

For such reasons, no doubt, at the beginning of 1998, the then Chairman of S4C, Prys Edwards, announced to an expectant world that the language war was over. Quite a lot of people thought that was coming it a bit strong, but at the same time the statement wasn't dismissed as a piece of over-dressed public relations flim-flam, which might have been its fate some years before. It was impossible to escape the thought, though, that while Welsh language campaigners can clearly point to some stirring victories, the policies of successive Governments in giving them largely what they wanted, admittedly grudgingly at times, had also paid off. The noise has subsided, and it was interesting to see that, when a row broke out over the linguistic standards of a re-launched Radio Cymru, the most ferocious critics weren't rebellious youths but, by and large, old buffers.

At the same time as the language appears to have become less of a threat, the image of Plaid Cymru has changed too. It's always been essentially a middle-class party and for that reason was at one time all the more anxious to make thunderous declarations of socialism and republicanism. Now, though, its bourgeois respectability is plain for all to see. It has two solicitors, a former industrial executive and an ex-teacher of English as its MPs. Its President is distinguished by a significant British honour, being the Rt Hon Dafydd Wigley, a Privy Councillor and so officially an adviser to the Queen. His former colleague, Dafydd Elis Thomas, now Lord Elis-Thomas of Nant Conwy, was sent to the House of Lords by a Conservative Prime Minister, and took on the chairmanship of a substantial quango, the Welsh Language Board, at a rate of £22,290 a year for a two-day week. Sometimes I have to pinch myself to make sure I'm not dreaming, as such people drop into line behind the establishment they once excoriated from every platform they could find.

Not that they present it like that. Dafydd Elis Thomas, who once liked nothing better than to talk over a good lunch about something called mobilising the Welsh working class, can still look on it as a version of fighting behind enemy lines. "Unfortunately in the UK we have these stupid titles and so you can't become a member of the second chamber without accepting this silly title," is his version. "Nor can you become an MP without swearing an oath of allegiance to the Queen. You can refuse to swear an allegiance to God but you can't get away from the Royal Family because she's head of state and so there are these conventions which, if you're going to do something in the institution, you have to accept."

Oh, I see.

Most people still don't vote for Plaid Cymru, but it seems to me that the way in which they've blended with the political background has diminished the terror that made people like George Thomas reach for a crucifix and some garlic whenever the word nationalism entered the political debate. The party is certainly respectable, even, when you think about it, mainstream. And I think it's possible to argue that that sort of change, and with it the reduced sensitivity of the language issue, were among the important influences on the outcome of the 1997 referendum. Much more significant than either, though, was the fact that there had been a previous disastrous gallop round this course – in the referendum of March 1, 1979.

Once the Welsh voters had on that occasion unceremoniously dumped what was literally intended to be, you might say, a Labour-saving device, and a couple of months later the British electorate had done the same to the Government, I assumed that that was the last I'd see of the matter in my lifetime, although I was well under forty at that stage. I was wrong because I didn't realise then that once you have opened the constitutional box and looked inside, it's virtually impossible to get the lid back on. You have raised expectations which sooner or later have to be fulfilled in some way. That referendum and its failure, we can see now, made a significant contribution to the process of inventing Wales and Welsh politics. Everyone was involved in it, even if sometimes they pretended they weren't. And it's in this category that we find the contribution made by the Conservative Party in Wales.

In 1970, Peter Thomas became the first Tory to be Secretary of State for Wales and, despite the party's opposition to the very existence of the job, the Conservatives showed no inclination to abolish it. Quite the reverse, as we were to discover as we went along. At that time, though, the party's overall strategy assumed that the progress or otherwise of Wales was a more or less mechanical consequence of United Kingdom policies. It was, after all, the Conservative and Unionist Party, and if historically that title referred to Ireland, it reflected a view that took in Wales and Scotland as well.

In those days the Conservatives' Welsh conference was a perfunctory affair, with retired majors, their wives, a few businessmen and a lawyer or two making up a large part of the audience which would pop along to Llandrindod Wells on a summer Saturday to sit in the *Metropole Hotel* agreeing how good the party leadership was. They would stage a couple of

low-key discussions, share afternoon tea and still be home in
time for that pre-dinner gin and tonic.

We journalists had to turn up and make of it what we could,
which wasn't very much. But then it suddenly struck the
Conservatives that other political parties, chiefly Labour but an
increasingly energetic Plaid Cymru as well, were getting much
more publicity than they were because their conferences somehow seemed more interesting, not to mention longer.

Having woken up to the possibilities of what a real conference
might deliver, the Tories, being very skilled professional political
operators then largely untroubled by namby-pamby questions
like internal party democracy, decided they should have a better
event than anyone else. The result was a well-attended, highly-
disciplined annual meeting at which senior figures would be
cheered to the echo as they made important-sounding speeches
and Cabinet Ministers would form a docile queue in the street
as they waited to be interviewed by someone from HTV or
BBC Wales.

The consequence of this wasn't simply all that delicious
publicity. If you had a Welsh party conference then you had to
talk about Welsh issues, even if the best you could do was to
pass resolutions agreeing that the breathtaking brilliance of the
Government's overall policies was just what Wales needed. But
then, soon afterwards, the Heath Government was defeated and
Labour arrived with its plans for an elected Welsh assembly. On
that basis the Conservatives had to have at least one specific
policy for Wales whether they wanted to or not. So it was that
on the Saturday morning of the June 1974 conference, Peter
Thomas, by then Shadow Secretary of State, announced the
details of the Tories' own Welsh devolution plans. That afternoon, Ted Heath turned up and announced them all over again.
The details of what they had to say needn't detain us here, the
point was that they were now fully involved in the game, they
actually had some plans, however tentative and uninspiring they
might be.

Even so, it would be wrong to give the impression that this
was the Conservative Party's first real involvement in Welsh
politics rather than in politics in Wales. After all, it was Winston
Churchill himself who created the Welsh Office in 1951 and

not, as is often mistakenly said, Harold Wilson in 1964. Wilson simply upgraded it by creating the Cabinet post of Secretary of State. It began life as part of the Home Office and, while this might have been seen as a way of being nice to the Welsh, it also had something of a colonialist tinge about it. It was a recognition by the Government that there were such things as Welsh affairs and that they needed ministers to attend to them. And since a sense of national identity has got as much to with who you're not as who you are, it meant that there were outsiders on whom to focus discontent: English Cabinet Ministers, Tories, people you'd never heard of, people who were not Welsh telling Welsh people what to do.

Thus when responsibility for Wales passed to the Ministry of Housing and Local Government, the Minister, Henry Brooke, quickly became a hate figure in some quarters. The contradictions contained in his dual role were starkly revealed when he, as Minister for Local Government, gave permission for the building of the Tryweryn reservoir to provide water for the people of Liverpool. The flooding of the Merionethshire valley involved and the drowning of the village of Capel Celyn took on an iconic status in Wales, and not only for nationalists.

Under his other hat as Minister for Wales though, Brooke didn't even bother arguing the point with himself. Forty years later it is not only impossible to imagine a Welsh Office minister giving permission for such a scheme, it is unthinkable that such a scheme would ever be put forward for ministerial consideration. It is one measure of the way in which the relationship between Wales and the United Kingdom has changed in that time, regardless of the success or otherwise of devolution proposals.

Anyway, the ball was rolling. In 1957, the first specifically Welsh minister was appointed, again by a Conservative Government. As has often been the case, Tory Party talent in Wales was rather thin on the ground so they found a Breconshire councillor called Vivian Lewis, sent him to the House of Lords where, as Lord Brecon, he became Minister of State for Welsh Affairs. Looking at this process it's enticing to think that it was Winston Churchill, much reviled in Wales, who was the begetter of a Welsh assembly. He was certainly one of them because, from those modest beginnings in 1951, the administration of Wales has become a vast industry. After all, there are now far more civil servants on the surface in the Welsh Office than there are miners underground. But no administration, whatever its colour or professed convictions, has made any attempt to reverse the process or even slow it down.

In 1964 the Conservatives didn't want a Secretary of State in the Cabinet at all, but nevertheless consistently found him new things to do when it was their turn. When, in 1967, Cledwyn Hughes produced proposals for the reform of local government in Wales (with an elected all-Wales council discreetly slipped into the plan) he was told everyone would have to wait and see what was suggested for England. Twenty-five years later a Conservative Secretary of State was cheerfully reorganising local government pretty well regardless of what was being done elsewhere.

The Labour Party busily created quangos as a complement to the Welsh Office (the Welsh Development Agency, the Development Board for Rural Wales and the Land Authority for Wales in the seventies, for example) and afterwards spent all their time complaining that the Tories were running them. Nicholas Edwards, as Shadow Secretary of State, regularly issued warnings that these organisations weren't long for this world. When his time came, though, he didn't harm a hair on the head of one of them, but instead found some under-employed Conservatives to take control.

This was not much of a change in the status quo since Labour had previously found places for failed politicians (Gordon Parry, who lost to Edwards in Pembroke, and Ednyfed Hudson-Davies on his journey from seat to seat and party to party, at the Tourist Board, for example) and superannuated trade union officials (Sir David Davies of the Iron and Steel Trades Confederation was the first chairman of the WDA), while the Conservatives favoured businessmen with time on their hands, or ex-officers like Colonel (now Sir) Geoffrey Inkin who eventually got to chair not one large quango but two, the Cardiff Bay Development Corporation and the Land Authority for Wales. It would probably be unfair to describe Inkin as a failed politician as well since a single outing as the Conservative

candidate for Ebbw Vale can hardly be considered a sign of insatiable ambition for elected office.

In another twist to this process the former Montgomery MP, Emlyn (now Lord) Hooson was rejected for the Welsh National Governorship of the BBC because Mrs Thatcher didn't want public office to give any kind of credibility to the Liberal Party. She didn't mind offering it to a Labour politician, Cledwyn Hughes (now Lord Cledwyn of Penrhos), but he turned it down, perhaps on the grounds that it wasn't quite elevated enough for a man of his achievement and distinction.

The point is that this is how political parties, all of them, go about their daily business, and whenever you hear them moralising over such questions it's best to check the cat to see if it's laughing. At the same time, when the public became aware of some of the things that were going on, notably in the scandals that beset the WDA in the nineties, they could have been forgiven for wondering if this was the best system man could devise for regulating public enterprise. It was another area where people began using words like accountability.

It was under the Edwards regime, too, that we began to understand the difference between what governments say they are doing and what they are actually up to. One of the central Thatcher principles was that there was to be no state intervention in private industry of the kind which had been carried out by the National Enterprise Board. The NEB was wound up soon enough but the WDA, which was in part its Welsh equivalent, took a short pause for breath before, under Edwards's supervision, it was busily intervening away as if there'd never been an election. Whoever was in charge, the Welsh Office increasingly had a life of its own, particularly after the introduction (again under Edwards) of the block grant system, something which meant it had much more influence on the allocation of public spending.

At the same time there has perhaps been as much significance in the way the Welsh Office runs things as in what it runs. It has to do with the size of Wales and the fact that practically everyone in political and public life knows practically everyone else. That doesn't necessarily mean they like each other (read Edwards's book on the failure to build the Cardiff Bay opera house if you're in any doubt) but they often have a common purpose and a common interest in getting things done. This emerges clearly in relationships between the Welsh Office and local government, especially when you remember that Labour councillors, who run most of the authorities, are frequently people who think a deal well negotiated is at least as important as pursuing some distant socialist goal, even assuming such a thing would be permitted these days. This has meant, for example, that the sour atmosphere which often characterises relations between English local authorities and the Department of the Environment has been largely absent from Wales.

Nor is this new. When the Heath Government introduced the Housing Finance Act in 1972 which forced councils to increase council house rents, some local authorities in both England and Wales set out on a policy of non-implementation. In England the result was confrontation between councils and the government during which, most famously, members of Clay Cross in Derbyshire were surcharged by the district auditor and barred from office. In Wales, two authorities, Merthyr and Bedwas and Machen, refused to obey the legislation. The Secretary of State, Peter Thomas, chose a different route from that taken by his English counterpart. He sent commissioners into the two councils specifically to take over the running of housing and nothing else.

In this way in Wales there was no serious conflict between councillors and the government or, more important, between councillors and the law. Honour was satisfied all round. Their protest had been made but had also been neatly circumvented without the need for the big stick. And in contrast to Clay Cross, there was no continuing grievance to be dealt with when Labour returned to power in 1974, followed by a residual sense of resentment that the government couldn't retrospectively lift all the penalties involved.

Thus it was that a row between Labour authorities and a Conservative government caused more trouble for Labour than it did for the Tories, an outcome fairly typical of the way in which the Labour Party conducted itself in those days. The fact that at that time the MP for Bolsover, which included Clay Cross, was Dennis Skinner, the implacable leftie and Commons entertainer, and that his brother was one of the councillors involved, may tell us something. The fact that at the same time the Leader of Bedwas and Machen Council (and later in the affair, housing committee chairman) was Ron Davies who, in 1997, became Secretary of State for Wales, may tell us something else.

It is also the case in Wales that the most serious disputes take place between members of the Labour Party who are capable of confronting each other with a passion and implacable zeal which makes the Cold War look like a game of beach cricket. These disputes rarely have anything to do with political principle but rather with winning and losing, with control. So it was entirely predictable that when Valleys Labour, in the shape of Ron Davies, came up against Cardiff Labour, as represented by Russell Goodway, Leader of the City Council, it would be absolutely impossible to reach agreement on installing the Welsh Assembly in the City Hall, something which had all along been considered to be a fait accompli. You could have bet your house on there being trouble and still slept easily at night.

In an atmosphere of deals where party was often less important than personality, Conservative Secretaries of State could feel as much at ease as their Labour counterparts, and they have taken some pleasure in the sense in which they can, in however small a way, make a difference to events. As on the occasion, for example, when a financial crisis at Welsh National Opera was instantly solved by David Hunt finding a spare few hundred thousand pounds from somewhere. There is no politician born who doesn't like to get on the telly announcing good news, if possible the same good news three or four times, and in Wales it doesn't cost all that much. They like the cosiness of it, too, the sense that Wales is a kind of ideal, bite-sized political unit, even though the Conservatives have always resisted what is presented as the next logical step – to run more of it from within Wales itself. Nevertheless, they have contributed as much as anyone to the currency of that idea which, again, was much more in tune with the mood of the nineties than it was with that of the seventies.

It's a curious thing, though, that running the Welsh Office, well or badly, hasn't brought much by way of rewards elsewhere. It's not for nothing that it's earned a reputation as the

Bermuda Triangle of British political life, a place where high-fliers suddenly disappear from the radar screens and are never heard of again, no-one more sensationally, of course, than Ron Davies. One or two seem to have moved upwards, only for the curse of Cathays Park to descend on them when they least expect it. David Hunt, for example, known as Dai Delighted because of the Rotarian bonhomie with which he approached his tasks – his presentational skills, in the jargon of the day – did get another couple of Cabinet jobs. But after the disastrous period when John Major decided to put himself up for election to a post he already held, Hunt suddenly realised that he was by now actually the man in charge of the Government's image and it wasn't a very good one. The consequence was that he declined further office on the grounds of his own failure – a rare moment of self-awareness in a politician.

But what about William Hague? people will say. Well, we shall see. What about John Redwood, then? I certainly wouldn't put the milk money on his future career. Although it was a minor incident in itself, it's impossible to escape the persistent image of the complete hash he made of not just failing to sing *Mae Hen Wlad Fy Nhadau*, but of failing even to *mime* it convincingly, with the cameras capturing every excruciating moment. Despite the big brain of which we have heard so much, he looked clumsy and embarrassed and entirely out of touch with the political world he wished to dominate. If a politician can't fake it, frankly, he's in trouble, something compounded in this instance by the fact that malevolent broadcasters proceeded to dig out the tape every few months and remind people once more about an incident which was both richly comic and cruelly revealing.

Perhaps this was one of the events that made Welsh people feel more warmly about devolution, but there was another way in which Redwood contributed in a significant manner to the debate. The Welsh Office is supposed to be a dead-end job (Kenneth Baker fled from public life rather than take it) but it has one significant advantage over most other ministries. The holder is in the enviable position of being legitimately able to comment on any of the big political and social issues of the day without being accused of interfering in other people's business.

The remit of the department is so wide that there is scarcely any aspect of human life for which the Secretary of State cannot claim some responsibility. Redwood might not have been the first to recognise this, but he was the first to exploit it with such vigour.

On July 2, 1993, not much more than a month after he had joined the Cabinet, Redwood made his famous speech about the St Mellons housing estate in Cardiff, in which he expressed surprise at the number of single-parent families there. "In that community," he said, "people have begun to accept that babies just happen and there is no presumption in favour of two adults creating a loving family background for their children. It is that which we have to change."

In the book *Guilty Men*, in which Hywel Williams, Redwood's political adviser at the Welsh Office, presents a caustic and unflattering portrait of his former boss, it emerges that this apparently unexceptional piece of sermonising was unpopular with John Major for a number of reasons. At this stage the Prime Minister was preparing to launch his "Back to Basics" campaign; Redwood's speech not only upstaged that, but its chilly puritanism struck a note the government were particularly anxious to avoid. Given the extent of the fornication and dishonesty which then preoccupied so many Conservative MPs that was a shrewd piece of judgement, but it was in part wrecked by this kind of self-righteousness. In a matter of weeks in the Welsh Office Redwood had established himself as a man of high moral sensibilities, a big thinker and an independent spirit. No wonder he kept on doing it.

Later that year he made a speech on the Health Service which did little to disguise the fact that he believed he had a much better idea of how to run it than did people like Virginia Bottomley, the then Health Secretary. There was hardly a subject on which he could not and did not pronounce, explaining what he was doing 'in Wales', but all the time implying that this was how they ought to do it in the rest of the United Kingdom and, indeed, that he was just the chap to do it. It was an astonishing performance by any standards and through it Redwood achieved the unthinkable: he became a famous Secretary of State for Wales, detested by the Prime Minister rather than ignored by him, which had long been the tradition. And in getting to this elevated position he drew people's attention to the nature of the Welsh Office, the way it operated and its influence in their lives. For this reason it's possible to argue that John Redwood did as much as anyone to awaken a public, which had been catatonic with indifference in 1979, to some of the central issues of the devolution debate. As what you might call a British nationalist he would no doubt find this deeply depressing.

All these things that I've so far mentioned have probably made some contribution to the shift of opinion in Wales, however tentative, that brought us to our present position. But what has really changed is politics itself and politicians with it. What we have seen, with one notable exception, is the break-up of consensus, a period of turbulence in which it seemed that things would never be the same again, and then the re-establishment of consensus in a form which is at the same time recognisable and unfamiliar.

I became the BBC's Welsh Political Correspondent in 1970, a sign of the times, perhaps, since I was the first person to hold that title. Maybe, as I'll explore later, the BBC was giving Welsh politics a bit of a prod, while at the same time Welsh politics was giving the BBC a nudge. They didn't go all the way at once: I was also the industrial correspondent, which largely meant labour correspondent, which in its turn meant strikes correspondent. It was believed that for many years the BBC refused to give anyone the title, common in newspapers, of Labour Correspondent, in case there was an immediate demand for a Conservative Correspondent as well. Nowadays such people are known as industry correspondents or business affairs correspondents, something with a ring of the oak-panelled boardroom about it, anyway, rather than of the shop floor.

This diversion into nomenclature isn't as trivial as it might seem at first sight because, to a large extent, it represented the divisions that then characterised politics: workers against owners, socialism against capitalism, words on which, as I write them, I can see the moss growing. The Labour Party stood for public ownership, increased public spending, particularly on welfare, and free collective bargaining. The Conservatives said they believed in private enterprise, lower public spending and restrictions on the trades unions' rights of industrial action. On the whole, though, the two parties ended up doing more or less the same things.

The Conservative Party certainly didn't do anything about privatising the nationalised industries. Quite the reverse in fact, and as early as 1971 Heath was taking Rolls Royce into public ownership to save it from ignominious collapse. Public spending was cut, only to be increased again shortly afterwards in an attempt to find a way out of economic stagnation. Everyone thought a pay policy was a waste of time, but one was introduced, just as Wilson had done previously and Callaghan was to do later. Under Wilson, Barbara Castle had failed to get Cabinet support for plans to restrict the powers of the unions. Heath got his legislation through, but not only did it cause trouble rather than alleviate it, but in the end he was fatally damaged by two strikes, both by the National Union of Mineworkers, and both of which were entirely legal. Government and Opposition officially disagreed over Europe but each had a substantial minority who were perfectly prepared to defy the party line.

In these circumstances, one of the few things that looked even vaguely like a radical policy was that which brought Margaret Thatcher to public attention for the first time. As Education Secretary she decided to save a few million pounds by ending the supply of free school milk to children between the ages of eight and eleven. This caused great outrage, particularly in Wales where a lot of political debate consists of the exchange of deprivation statistics between the parties, and it was treated as though she were proposing that small children should once more be sent to work underground.

"Thatcher the Milk Snatcher," they jeered, as Merthyr council in particular fought an enterprising battle against the edict, claiming at one time that while the law might say they weren't allowed to provide free milk, it didn't say anything about free milk *shakes*. No-one took too much notice of the fact that it had been a Labour government which had taken school milk from older children.

Spool on through the tempestuous years of the seventies,

eighties and nineties and once again you find yourself with a government accused of neglecting the welfare of the poor, this time through cuts in benefits. Public spending must be kept under strict control, nothing is to be re-nationalised and the unions must fend for themselves as best they can. There is a pay policy in force, formal in the public sector, informal in the private. The Opposition, while trying not to say so, agrees with most of this. Both main parties disagree over Europe and both have substantial minorities opposed to the party line.

This is a remake, not a new movie, and in these circumstances it's not surprising that the baffled voter wonders about the system by which he is governed. But he has another problem because, while all this has been going on, the Wales he knew thirty years ago, even twenty years ago, has largely disappeared from under his feet. Confronted with an industrial and social revolution introduced by a Conservative Government which was for so many years apparently unassailable, Opposition politicians have inevitably turned their minds to other sources of power. Outwards to the European institutions is one direction in which they've looked. Many, too, have taken some faltering steps to what Michael Foot commended to a Welsh Labour Party conference in the seventies as "a measure of self-government".

"A measure of self-government?" was the scalding response from his friend Neil Kinnock. "You might as well talk about a measure of pregnancy." Kinnock doesn't say that now, of course. The man who once denounced Brussels before breakfast six days a week is now at the heart of its bureaucracy as one of the British members of the European Commission. The man who fought his own party to a standstill over devolution believes that, in what he carefully calls the context of devolved government throughout Britain, a Welsh assembly will be essentially a good thing.

Some people are inclined to criticise Kinnock for these changes of view. That's particularly true in those sections of the Labour Party where a single idea is supposed to be enough to last you a lifetime, even in the face of incontrovertible evidence that it's not a very good idea. But Kinnock's views demand at least a hearing because, as Leader, he was one of the lifeboatmen who pulled Labour off those rocks of ideological disaster.

The central problem he eventually identified lay in a crucial distinction you can apply equally well to subjects like devolution and the European Union as much as to the fundamental aims of the party.

"We didn't distinguish between means and ends," he said. "We thought the definition of socialism was nationalisation and, of course, the definition is much more than that. That was just one instance of thinking that the means of securing public ownership was an end in itself and I think that misled a lot of us for many, many years. We made a shibboleth of a particular system of organising the economy with the result that we reduced our number of friends and we made unnecessary enemies."

Out on the left, where realism was a dirty word, making enemies and losing friends used to be taken as a pretty certain indicator that you'd got things right and, just because something didn't work, it certainly didn't mean you'd got it wrong. It just meant that the forces of reaction were ranged against you as usual. Neil Kinnock used to live out there and, like a lot of people in the Labour Party, he's made a long journey. People of his kind used to argue with some force that if you wanted to tackle the problems of Wales you needed centralised planning and direction by a British state itself in control of the commanding heights of the economy. But neither under Labour nor the Conservatives did such a regime prevent the de-industrialisation of much of Britain thanks to failures of foresight, nerve and resources, as we all witnessed in those communities in Wales which depended, for example, on coal or steel or textiles.

Once you begin to accept, like Kinnock, that one of the central political principles in which you've long believed – like public ownership – is fatally flawed, then all other aspects of policy are up for re-examination, including the methods by which we are governed. Some people have long argued (not all that many, admittedly) that Wales would have made a much better fist of it economically if it had been able to manage its own business. In times when traditional treatments fail people tend to look for alternative therapies and Plaid Cymru perhaps got a slightly larger audience than usual when it talked about Sweden or Ireland or Catalonia and said Wales would be richer if it ran its own affairs. (It's interesting, by the way, that no-one ever says self-government is in itself so desirable that it would be worth being a bit poorer to achieve it, a point of view that might carry rather more moral force but not all that many votes.) I don't think anyone really believes, as I've heard suggested, that if Wales had had self-government, the pits wouldn't have closed. That's an extreme response to the failures of central government and a romantic one at that, but the history of the last thirty years has perhaps attracted more people to the idea that they might themselves do something further to influence their own destiny. As least it couldn't be worse, people sometimes muttered into their beer.

I wouldn't want to over-estimate the importance of such ideas and events but, taken together, the changes in attitude as well as in the social and industrial condition of Wales since the 1979 referendum, processes that have often gone hand-in-hand, do give some indication of how people's view of the world has been altered. The way in which they had accumulated was illustrated by a chance encounter, months before the vote, with a Conservative who had served many years in local government. He surprised me when he said: "There's going to be a Welsh assembly and I want to be in it." That statement marked the first time I thought there might, just, be a 'yes' vote, although the fact that it came as a revelation might also reveal quite a lot about my skills as a political seer.

Other people who are paid to know these things could quite clearly sense an altered mood. The CBI, which had been among the leaders of the opposition to the 1979 proposal, expressed doubts but took no corporate line. It was a recognition, I think, that if there was a good chance of being on the losing side it would be tactically astute to keep a low profile. The Conservatives in Wales didn't campaign officially against an assembly, presumably on the grounds that, in the light of the May election when it won no seats in Wales, to do so would be to guarantee a huge majority in favour, as well as providing further evidence of how out of touch the party was.

As well as new attitudes, though, what was needed was some good, old-fashioned, political fixing, a skill prized above most others by the new Labour Government. If you're interested in how things get done you simply have to stand back and admire the strategy which brought us a Scottish referendum on September 11 and a Welsh one on September 18. The Scottish result told us that the nature of government in Britain was changing there and then. The driver had taken the handbrake off and the conductor had already pressed the bell when Wales took a flying leap on to the platform, aware that it would be left behind, and that there might not be another bus along for ten years, maybe longer. Me-tooism is a powerful force in politics, something the Labour Cabinet and spin doctors had shrewdly recognised.

On the morning of September 19, the three Welsh Office Ministers stood on the platform at the Welsh College of Music and Drama in Cardiff, holding hands aloft with those of the leaders of Plaid Cymru and the Welsh Liberal Democrats. If you're sometimes tempted to think that nothing much has changed in politics, buy a picture of that and stick it on the wall. In the middle Ron Davies, whose political career had been written off a dozen times that night by commentators and opponents, might then have said in reply, as Disraeli once did, that a majority is the best repartee.

What did it matter if the eventual majority could have been put in a Marks and Spencer's plastic bag and carried away without effort by a small child? A decision which would inevitably change the nature of Wales had effectively been taken by a quarter of the voters. Suppose, for instance, it had rained all day in Carmarthen, what then? Well, it didn't. There were protests to come, as much about arithmetic as about the unsatisfactory nature of the democratic process, but there is an unyielding decisiveness about the ballot box.

And legitimacy: one of the problems with much of the referendum campaign in Wales seemed to me that it was conducted at an essentially trivial level. It will cost a lot of money, opponents would say. No it won't, came the unhelpful reply, but no-one was willing to risk examining the proposition that if it was worth having, it would be worth paying for. Members of the "How Many?" school of political analysis had a wonderful time, trying to work out how many hip replacements or new classrooms, or day centres could be paid for if the money concerned didn't go to the assembly. This is the sort of disreputable argument that gives even politics a bad name.

Others said that, confronted by yet more bureaucracy, foreign companies would place their investments elsewhere. This ignored the fact that some of the most significant names in world industry – Sony and Panasonic, for example – built factories in Wales during the seventies when a Labour Government was not only attempting to set up a Welsh assembly, but was actually so unreconstructed that it still had plans for further nationalisation.

Then again, it would lead to the break-up of the United Kingdom, or jealous English MPs would take an axe to the funding formula which gives Wales slightly more public spending than its weight strictly allows. The assembly would not be satisfied with its minimal powers and there would be endless conflict between Cardiff and Westminster. Some or all of these assertions might turn out to be true, but often they were not rebutted by argument but met instead with populist sloganising which emphasised in particular the view that devolution represented an extension of democracy. Democracy is, as we all know, a good thing, and more of it is therefore an even better thing and anyone who argues against that is clearly an authoritarian bigot.

However, the kind of debate – or non-debate – on which the parties seemed to settle during the campaign raises one of the central issues about the future of Wales under the new dispensation. Democracy isn't simply about how many times you vote or the nature of structures which are put in place to be run by politicians. It is also about knowledge, and a detailed understanding of who governs us and how they do it. Those six thousand seven hundred and twenty-one votes on September 18, I believe, have now made that a vital question too, perhaps even the most important question now facing Wales.

Outside Looking In

Isuppose the most shameful episode in which I have been involved in more than thirty years in journalism was the occasion on which I found myself forced, in a single phrase, to reveal the insecure foundations on which the whole trade is often constructed. It happened in the early summer of 1969 when assorted fantasists and amateur insurrectionists were assembled in the dock at Swansea Assizes and accused of various offences committed during their existence as what was known as the Free Wales Army, an organisation whose history tells us a great deal about the nature of journalism in Wales and elsewhere. Among other things, for example, it provides an illustration of the way in which unenterprising journalists feel their way from one cliché to another with the aid of nothing more sophisticated than a white stick.

The story at that time was that a disaffected Wales was on the verge of boiling over into an armed rebellion. It was a story without a shred of truth in it, but truth is by no means the first concern of editors, and perhaps their readers, who often want the world described as they would like it to be rather than as it is. And very often that means worse than it really is, rather than better. That's why, after all, loonies, monsters and fiends relentlessly stalk the pages of the tabloid press every day, although in reality there are hardly enough of them to go round.

The Free Wales Army represented what newspapers wanted to be the truth and from there it was only a short step to it being the truth. In the case of Wales this is a process often given a greater impetus by the journalistic formula of an inverse correlation between the distance from London of an event and the need to describe it with any accuracy. This is further reinforced by the theory that there's no point in going all that way to discover that people are more or less the same as you are or, even worse, more or less the same as your news editor.

So it was that a handful of men and a large dog, all holding the rank of commandant including, perhaps, the dog, would put on comic opera uniforms and march through places like

Machynlleth to the delight of jeering under-tens. Once, at the village of Cilmeri, where people gather to mark the death in 1282 of Llywelyn ap Gruffydd, considered by some to be the last authentic Prince of Wales, a small car was seen with a note on its windscreen: "Free Wales Army – gone to lunch".

Any journalist who cared to could get a blood-curdling threat for the price of a phone call. The more ridiculous the claims they made, the more eager were newspapers and magazines to print them. "Thousands are massing in the hills, ready to declare war on the British Government," one commandant or another would pronounce. "Thousands are massing in the hills, ready to declare war on the British Government," goggle-eyed and grateful journalists would scribble in their notebooks.

No story was considered too far-fetched to alarm jaded readers over their cornflakes in Godalming or Pinner, including the news that squads of dogs were being trained to carry magnetic mines. When the day came, we learned, they would be sent out to make the ultimate canine sacrifice and blow up English tanks as they crossed the border. This kamikaze effort would be accompanied, no doubt, by shouts of *bonzo* rather than *banzai*.

While this all seems pretty silly now it was given a certain amount of credibility at the time because of the tensions associated with preparations for that great Ruritanian event, the Investiture of the Prince of Wales. Bombs really were going off, nerves were frayed, something had to be done, someone had to be put on trial, a move which is often the nervous resort of baffled authorities. And who better to haul into court than the raggle-taggle mob whose threat to public order consisted almost entirely of their own announcements processed by the collective imagination of the British media?

The significance of what I had to say at their trial I'll come to in a little while, but it suited most people, particularly politicians and the police, to take the FWA at their own valuation, although you didn't have to be trained in forensic psychology to understand that while these chaps might have been barmy they were otherwise pretty harmless. There was, it was true, someone planting bombs, but it wasn't them, and eventually it was revealed that the man responsible for at least some of this activity, John Jenkins, was in fact a member of a real army – the British one. Not only that, but he was spending his evenings making the bombs with the dental mechanic's equipment with which he had been issued by the Ministry of Defence. Naturally enough he didn't go round announcing this to people so you couldn't read about it in the British press. This is no doubt why it took the police so long to get round to arresting him since it's much easier to catch offenders who proclaim their guilt to anyone who'll listen.

This failure of journalism to distinguish between fact and fantasy is less unusual today than it was then. Nowadays many papers can discern no dividing line between characters in television soap operas and those who have a physical reality. Sometimes even politicians, anxious to show how in touch they are with the everyday world of the average voter, are willing to pronounce on the fictional plight of non-existent people. Even someone as nakedly unsympathetic as Michael Howard once, as Home Secretary, commented on a gaol sentence passed on a character in *The Archers*. Are there no lengths to which such people will not go, you wonder, in their efforts to retain office?

But nineteen-sixties Wales was not the journalistic desert it was to become. Consequently it was rather more surprising that the story of the Free Wales Army should have been so imaginatively presented, because in that period most of the national newspapers had correspondents permanently based in Wales. Representatives of *The Times*, *The Daily Telegraph*, *The Guardian*, the *Daily Mail*, *The Sun* and the *Daily Express*, as well as the indefatigable man from the Press Association, were all on the spot, every day. Admittedly they weren't all over-employed, and at least one was believed to spend a substantial part of his week poring over a map of Wales deciding, for expenses purposes, where he would have gone if he had actually gone anywhere.

One way and another, though, there was a lot more journalism in Wales than there is now. Newspaper editors and proprietors thought it a proper part of their business to maintain such people in Wales, even if their main interest was in violent crimes, sensational trials and large-scale industrial disputes of which in those days there were quite a number. And if some were more enterprising than others, if they went out and discovered Wales or even invented it, their work would very likely find a place somewhere in their papers. Now, though, in the age of the internet, the fax machine, the mobile phone and all the other trinkets associated with the information revolution, people a hundred and fifty miles away up the M4 are less likely to know than they were then what is going on in Wales. So, for that matter, are people in Wales itself.

Quite a lot of modern journalism is a process in which a writer finds convenient ways of reinforcing his prejudices and preconceptions. It is for such reasons that Tower Colliery at Hirwaun, the last gasp of a once huge coal industry, has become such a magnet for feature writers from around the country. It is a romantic story, of course, men backing themselves against the inexorable processes of geology and state capitalism, but it is also a story outsiders find it easy to grasp: if it's Wales, it must be coal, see.

So it was that the retired politician and Stakhanovite scribbler, Roy Hattersley, now Lord Hattersley, popped down to Hirwaun one day to write a piece for the *Mail on Sunday*. He could hardly believe his luck. He wrote excitedly: 'The visitor expects Nerys Hughes to appear suddenly at the colliery gate – hugely maternal behind her long striped apron as she carries her batch of freshly-baked lava [*sic*] bread to the chapel social.'

Not long after this was published I was appearing on a radio programme with Hattersley and I mentioned that some people in Wales had been critical of that particular sentence in his piece. He got quite shirty (although very amusing, Hattersley is not as invariably filled with goodwill as you might imagine, particularly when it comes to those less celebrated than himself) and he said that of course he hadn't really expected Nerys Hughes to appear. Then he went on for a few minutes about Keith Waterhouse's idea that there should be an ironic typeface so that simple-minded people who were unaccountably allowed to read your imaginative and carefully-structured prose wouldn't think you meant literally every word you wrote.

All this took some time, and he was so clearly put out by the implication that he didn't know what he was doing that, in the end, I didn't have the heart to tell him that the problem wasn't with Nerys Hughes, lazy though the image was, but with the laver (or lava, as he thought) bread. No doubt he was under the impression that the ingredients were gathered at dawn by nimble-footed virgins in scanty peasant costumes scrambling about the volcanic slopes of the Gower Peninsula. How could I tell him that it was made of seaweed and best eaten fried, with bacon?

But there we are, sheer bloody ignorance isn't a crime, any more than the duchess syndrome ("How very quaint, did you make it yourself?") that affects the average laptop-carrying visitor. A few years ago a lady journalist (I use the expression 'lady journalist' because in her article you can almost hear the white gloves being pulled on) turned up in Wales to see the novelist Kingsley Amis, who was on his annual summer visit to Swansea. Amis gave her quite a hard time, something he was quite capable of without being prompted or provoked. But, given that he had just injured his back in a fall, that one of his closest friends had just died, that he was ill and, indeed, was to die within the next couple of months, in these circumstances it's hardly surprising that he didn't come on like the Queen of the May.

The intrepid writer, though, clearly didn't feel the initiative she had shown in turning up at all had been treated with sufficient respect. She wrote in *The Daily Telegraph*: "It isn't often one goes from London to Swansea to meet a famous figurehead and encounters such a lack of civility for one's pains."

The first thing to be said about this, of course, is that it isn't very often that a journalist goes from London to Swansea at all, even to meet a figurehead, an understandable inertia given that it is a pretty testing three-hour journey by train. But this also raises a very important professional question. How far from London should you be expected to go to be met with a lack of civility? If you get as far west as, say, Ealing, will you put up with withering contempt? Will you tolerate a certain amount of off-handedness at Reading? Will you insist, if you happen to make it through the Severn Tunnel, on being treated with fawning respect and undisguised admiration for your steadfast courage, as if you'd paddled up the Limpopo in a hollowed-out tree trunk?

It's particularly significant that this episode should concern Kingsley Amis, because he illustrates another of the problems encountered by those people who, described as outsiders, write about Wales. Amis had a good ear and a considerable instinct for what would upset people, both valuable gifts in a writer. He knew Wales well. Not only had he spent thirteen years from 1949 as a lecturer at the university in Swansea, but even after that he was a frequent visitor. During the summers he and assorted reprobate Welsh friends would sometimes travel in what he called a 'flexi-bus', a hired coach, from one Welsh source of lots of drink and food to another.

In later life, by the way, he used to put it about that he didn't really drink very much, that people greatly exaggerated his consumption as part of the Amis legend. All I can say is that the last time I met him, at a BBC lunch in 1993, where he arrived wearing what appeared to be a small marquee, he began proceedings with a large glass of neat gin, polished off quite a lot of Australian red and then said to our host: "Can I have a proper drink now?" A bottle of Scotch was fetched (a rare sight in the modern BBC) and Amis turned theatrically away as it was brought to him. "It's rude to look when other people are pouring," he said, as the golden liquid bubbled up towards the rim of the tumbler.

The point is, though, that his Welsh credentials were in order and his book, *That Uncertain Feeling*, published in 1955, is as good a comic novel about post-war Welsh life as you'll find, not least because comic novels about Welsh life at any period are quite thin on the ground. Perhaps it's because Amis was such a good reporter that some people took exception to his view of Wales, even if it were accurate, perhaps because it was accurate. Part of the native genius is for resenting the fact that people don't write about Wales and then resenting it all over again when they do. Sensitivity has reached such a pitch that journalists who are rude or abusive about Wales are routinely reported to the Race Relations Commission. This sort of thing is then described straight-faced in the newspapers and taken seriously by numbers of people who should know better including, unbelievably, the Race Relations Commission.

When *The Old Devils*, which won the Booker Prize, was

published in 1986, exception was taken to Amis's mockery of the Welsh language, the spelling of taxi as *tacsi*, for example, and various other manifestations of its state-sponsored public revival. At one point a character remarks: "Do you know they have wrestling in Welsh now on that new channel? Same as in English oddly enough except the bugger counts un – dau – tri etcetera. Then the idiots can go round saying the viewing figures for Welsh-language programmes have gone up. To four thousand and eleven."

While no-one in Welsh public life would be so foolhardy as to say such a thing these days, it's nevertheless only the small change of many discussions about the language among the minority which bothers to have them. The issue here is not whether it's right or wrong or appropriate or racist or anything else, but whether it is actually a view some people in Wales hold and even sometimes utter out loud. This is not some elaborate defence of Kingsley Amis the man. Many of his views were repellent: "See that nig-nog over there," he said quite loudly in the expensive London restaurant where I was trying to interest him in a radio programme. It was the first time we'd met and I wondered whether it was some kind of test, to see how I'd react, but if journalists went round reacting to things all day they'd never get any work done. But the 'what does he know?' school of literary criticism doesn't do any of us any favours if we are going to weed out all descriptions which don't coincide with those of the Wales Tourist Board. For example, Amis was no admirer of Dylan Thomas (who appears virtually undisguised as the dead poet Brydan in *The Old Devils*) either as a writer or as a human being, but he made an important point about him. It was that so powerful is Thomas's image and reputation, his myth, that he gets in the way of other writing about Wales.

He is such an oversized figure, in particular in the imagination of those who have never read a word he wrote, the literary equivalent of miners and male voice choirs, that people around the world can't be persuaded that there might be anything else going on, or ever has gone on, in the scribbling trade in Wales. His boyhood friend, the composer Daniel Jones, told me that strangers would turn up at his house at Newton, in Swansea, to ask him about Dylan. While Dan, who was very poor but both generous and polite, went to the kitchen to make a cup of tea, some of the visitors would steal his books, perhaps somehow to put themselves in closer touch, even at several removes, with the drunken poet who so extravagantly represents the image of Wales to a large part of the English-speaking world.

Even so, Amis's view of Dylan Thomas's literary merit or otherwise didn't prevent him accepting an invitation from his pal Stewart Thomas, an unappetising Swansea solicitor, to become a trustee of the Thomas literary estate. However, while visiting Laugharne one Sunday with another Swansea friend, Amis failed to negotiate some steps down to the beach and fell heavily on his bottom. By this stage of his life he was a vast figure who had severe difficulties in walking at all. It was in this way that he sustained the injury from which the lady from *The Daily Telegraph* found him suffering a few days later and which may well have precipitated his death. You don't have to believe too intensely in the paranormal to imagine that you could have heard ghostly laughter coming from Laugharne churchyard or, more likely, the bar of Brown's hotel.

Well, even if you don't like what Kingsley Amis wrote about Wales, at least he wrote something and, more than that, something which was neither insult nor fantasy. His case seems to me to underline one of the most important problems that confronts a changing Wales at the end of the twentieth century. How, from the outside as well as the inside, is it going to be described and describe itself? And it is not just the truth itself which is elusive, but the way in which we try and persuade ourselves and our readers about our authority and our accuracy. It was this question with which I was confronted in the summer of 1969 as the Free Wales Army Trial took its unhurried and expensive course at the Swansea law courts. I found myself, to put it bluntly, in the deeply embarrassing position of having to give the game away.

Eighteen months before, I had written a long article for *The Western Mail* about the FWA in which, being rather closer to the story than my Fleet Street brothers, I had taken a fairly sceptical line about the public pronouncements of the men who were to find themselves in the dock. The article, perhaps three thousand words long, filled a large part of an inside page and was headed with a blaring strapline: "A Special Investigation by Our News Focus Team."

Eventually one of the many barristers enjoying a lucrative summer at the seaside rose to ask me the killer question. "This News Focus team," he drawled, "Of whom did it consist?"

"Er... well... it was me, actually."

And so in a few moments I'd revealed the awful truth about the way in which journalists can create an alternative reality in a single bold sentence. "A special report" implies something arduously achieved at great expense. Even today it's a phrase frequently used by television news programmes to describe something longer and more boring than usual, saved up for a quiet news day. "Our news focus team" was of course intended to conjure up a picture of a whole room full of shirt-sleeved hacks tirelessly seeking the truth so that the Welsh public could sleep soundly at nights. In reality all this boiled down to one twenty-six-year-old journalist of limited experience taken off routine stories for a fortnight.

More important, perhaps, it revealed the gap between the glamorous aspirations of Welsh journalism and its threadbare reality. All right, then, all journalism, but Welsh journalism more than most. This was a period when investigative reporting, a very expensive commodity, was particularly fashionable, most famously in the *Insight* investigations for *The Sunday Times*. Others tried to match that as best they could. *The Times*, for instance, had something called The News Team, well-funded enough to arrive at one Welsh story in their own aircraft. *The Western Mail*'s version of in-depth journalism, in contrast, was *News Focus*, consisting of one man and a phone and for a time I wrote three a week.

What this cut-price version of the posh press represented, though, was another aspect of the chief characteristic of *The Western Mail* of those days which was the relentless search for information. Exclusives were highly prized, failure to get stories ahead of anyone else (especially the *South Wales Echo*, whose reporters sat in the same room) the source of constant reprimands. The news editor, John Humphries, who was later to edit the paper, was unmatched in his sleepless determination to squeeze the lemon of Welsh life until it had yielded every drop of what could be identified as news. Even by the manic standards of news editors the world over Humphries was hyper-active. I can see him now, crouched over the news desk, biro clenched in his fist, apparently threatening to stab his thick notebook to death as he chiselled in another few dozen numbered ideas for his reluctant reporters to follow up.

Greying hacks still swap stories about Humphries's unremitting work habits and the consequences for them of his sixteen-hour days, how tough men would stumble weeping from his presence, but in many ways he only represented an extravagantly driven version of journalism as it was practised throughout Britain at that time and which has now largely disappeared.

When I began work as a reporter on *The Luton News* in February 1964, the philosophy of the paper was that nothing moved in our circulation area without us publishing something about it. We had to. *The Luton News* was a thirty-two page broadsheet and it took a lot of filling. In addition to that we had the Beds and Herts *Saturday Telegraph* (not to mention the sporting edition – *The Green 'Un* – on Saturday evenings) demanding our attention as well.

The result was that no committee was too inconsequential, no careless driving case to trivial, no flower show too obscure, that it couldn't get its place in the paper. If the members of this or that parish council discussed street lighting well into the night, a man with a notebook would stay with them. A reporter would always be on hand to record the thunderous sermons on theft preached by magistrates who watched too much television. There was, too, a rigour about our work. We were on the spot when events took place, people were quoted with their names and addresses attached, never anonymously; there were none of those sources, insiders, senior officials, close friends or any of the other shadowy figures who flit through our newspapers every day. It was not until I became a correspondent some years later that I was allowed to use those weasel words of the hacking trade: "I understand".

Much of this has gone now. The network of information that it provided about British life has been dismantled. Large numbers of Britain's weekly newspapers have been turned into freesheets, most of which are overpriced even at nothing, while many of the dailies now concentrate their main efforts on what's known as lifestyle: lots of big pictures, a certain amount of news, quite a lot of material that purports to be news but isn't, some feature articles that look more like printing than journalism and, inevitably, columns by anyone who has worked out how to operate a keyboard. If you haven't got your mugshot at the head of a thousand words of whimsical prose then you must be the cleaner. There is, essentially, more icing than cake. This is not a process confined to what's known as the provincial press (*The Times*, for instance, has plunged downmarket with boyish enthusiasm) but it's much more significant in an area where there is so little competition.

In a sense it would be wrong to present this as a story of decline. It's a story of change, and a necessary one, as newspaper editors and proprietors struggle to produce something people will actually buy, but it is a process which has presented Wales in particular with a serious political problem. That is because it is taking place in a context in which newspaper journalism has a more important part to play in public life than ever before.

The Western Mail has long proclaimed itself to be the national newspaper of Wales but, as everyone knows, it is nothing of the kind, although why it is not tells us as much about Wales as it does about newspapers. The main problem is simple and intractable: geography. It is virtually impossible to make any kind of economic sense of printing a newspaper in Cardiff and selling it in sufficient numbers in North Wales. North of Aberystwyth *The Western Mail* has only a token readership and everyone else who wants Welsh news buys the Liverpool-based *Daily Post*. Every so often efforts have been made to change that, but they have inevitably ended in failure and retreat once the management realise, as one former editor put it, that they are pouring money down the drain.

Just as significant is the fact that people in North Wales are not particularly interested in what happens in South Wales, and vice-versa; many of them hardly ever make the journey south or north. The habitual directions taken, for business or pleasure, are east or west, something inevitably reflected in newspaper readership. Indeed, most people don't bother with

Welsh newspapers at all, and figures produced by the Institute of Welsh Affairs in 1996 showed that only thirteen per cent of the newspapers read by Welsh people were actually produced in Wales. Other readers will not find out much about Wales, I need hardly say, in the products of what used to be Fleet Street. There was, it is true, a brief flurry of interest in 1997, in the eight days between the result of the Scottish referendum and Glamorgan winning the county championship, but soon enough the footprints of the outside world had been washed from the sand. It then took a bizarre incident on Clapham Common more than a year later to put Wales back on the front pages.

But despite its failure to embrace the whole of Wales commercially, despite the fact that the vast majority of the population of Wales never read it, *The Western Mail* seems to me to have both reflected the way in which Wales has been re-shaped, invented really, and to have played a significant role in that process.

The paper's origins in 1869 were straightforwardly political. It was established by the trustees of the third Marquess of Bute as a direct result of a Conservative defeat in Cardiff in the previous year's election. In his book *Cardiff and the Marquesses of Bute*, the historian John Davies says that the blame was partly put down to the fact that the Conservatives had no powerful press support and so *The Western Mail* was founded to remedy the problem. When in 1877 it was sold to its editor, Lascelles Carr, it continued, Davies writes, "to advocate the causes which had been championed by the Bute estate since the time of the second marquess, combining staunch Conservatism and support for the Anglican establishment with wide coverage of Welsh cultural and national affairs."

It was to maintain that character for a long time, increasingly out of sympathy with the political and social realities of South Wales, something which provoked Aneurin Bevan to burn it publicly in the town square in Tredegar in 1926. As late as the sixties it retained a very conservative character, even if it was not overtly cheerleading for the Tories, but as what was essentially a journal of the establishment, particularly the business establishment, it probably felt that was the best, certainly the most discreet, course to take. In the seventies, however, events meant that it could no longer bury its head in the political sand. Like other organisations and individuals it had to make up its mind about the devolution question. In its way the paper's decision on what line to take was as important as the proposal itself, and the decision hinged on the chance of three or four significant personalities all coming to the same philosophical conclusion.

One of them was Duncan Gardiner who was the editor at the time. As a Yorkshireman, and the first Englishman to run the paper, he didn't carry the traditional Welsh political baggage about nationalism and any of its manifestations. At the same time, because he'd been a senior member of *The Western Mail* staff in the sixties, he knew the territory well. Among his lieutenants was Geraint Talfan Davies, an assistant editor who had been born into the Welsh media aristocracy and who was to become controller of BBC Wales at the end of the eighties. He is a man who has never for a second left anyone in any doubt about his enthusiasm for the creation and nurturing of Welsh institutions of all kinds. The chief leader writer was John Osmond, an obsessive devolutionist and one-man policy factory. "We combined together as a pretty good team on pushing the devolution line," Gardiner told me twenty years later. "It didn't necessarily meet with the approval of all the politicians, of course, and a lot of people accused us of being in the Welsh nationalist camp, which simply wasn't true."

There was one other important figure in this whose story is perhaps the most revealing of all: John Humphries, by then the paper's deputy editor. He had come into journalism by the traditional inky-fingered, school-leaver's route. For such reasons, and maybe others, he had more chips than Barry Island on an August weekend, suspicious to the point of paranoia of any authority except the hierarchy of newspapers, in particular of anyone who had had, or appeared to have had, his path smoothed through life, a category which included most graduates, civil servants, public relations officers, members of the Welsh establishment and, above all, members of the Welsh language establishment. Sometimes, at the end of the late nights we regularly worked, a group of us would talk our way into one of Cardiff's casinos where, over unbelievably expensive halves of bitter, Humphries would start arguments about who was middle class and so guilty of any number of unspecified offences.

"You have to remember what my background was," he told me many years afterwards. "I came from a line of terraced houses in Newport, and whereas I did go to a very good grammar school I don't think I was conscious of the Welsh language or of the Welsh nation until I was well and truly started in *The Western Mail*. In those days there was a certain hostility between the anglicised Welsh and the Welsh speakers. It was always felt there was some kind of conspiracy among the Welsh to ensure that they were always superior to the poor English speakers who were always in the majority. That, to my eternal regret, fed through my earlier years in journalism, but we all grow up.

"My attitude changed because I discovered my identity. Yes, I was Welsh born, I did have Welsh parents. I could identify with Welsh culture and the Welsh nation and I could even identify with the language. I became over the years one of the great supporters of the language, so much so that my eldest son is now a fluent Welsh speaker, having been a learner. Just recently I've had a first grandson and I'm sure the first words of that grandson will be Welsh."

No-one who had known him in the sixties would have believed that Humphries would embrace the cause of devolution with such passion, apart from the fact that he was clearly incapable of embracing any activity or idea except with passion. It seems to have been the devolution debates of the seventies that fired him to such an extent that he was eventually to become one of the leading campaigners, not simply for an assembly, but for a much more powerful Welsh parliament. But in there with his new view of Wales, questions of class persisted.

"I'd always been concerned in my earlier years in newspapers that some of the Welsh speakers were being groomed for stardom and this boy from a group of terraced houses in Newport becoming deputy editor had really bucked the trend. There was no way Geraint Talfan Davies or John Osmond were going to climb over me, because obviously I had my sights ultimately on becoming editor of *The Western Mail*, and I was to become editor of *The Western Mail* a decade later."

Such attitudes clearly created a feverish atmosphere along the editorial corridor of Thomson House, the paper's headquarters, as this disparate quartet tried to agree on a coherent policy. At one point in what was a long process, Humphries made up his mind that there was an overwhelming case for the Government's devolution proposals to be put to a referendum. His problem was how to get it past the others.

"By this time Duncan was frustrated by these endless discussions between these warring factions within the office. He decided there should be a showdown meeting at which he would decide whether the paper would support a referendum. He gave us all a week to prepare our cases."

At this point Geraint Talfan Davies contracted some illness and was not to be seen at the office. To Humphries this was a deeply sinister turn of events. "I was suspicious of a sickness at such a critical moment and I discovered from a secretary that, while Geraint truly was ill, he was also sitting up in bed preparing his opus on why *The Western Mail* should not support a referendum."

Ill or not, this manoeuvre seems to have somehow smacked of cheating in the great referendum contest. Davies, who is nothing if not thorough and now fortuitously free of office distractions, clearly had the time to prepare a detailed case. But Humphries, a streetfighter in such matters, turned this to his advantage. Geraint Talfan Davies's opportunity to prepare an exhaustive argument could be used against him.

"Knowing full well that my friend Duncan Gardiner would not read anything that ran to nine or ten pages of foolscap, I prepared my case for the referendum on a single foolscap sheet. When we met again and had the final showdown, Duncan had read mine thoroughly and we decided to support a referendum."

As it happens, that was a decision that Humphries came to regret, but its real significance lies in the fact that it was made at all, and made after such a thorough process of debate. It marked a shift in what *The Western Mail* saw as its proper role, indeed perhaps the most important change in its attitudes since the time the Marquess of Bute's trustees thought the Conservative Party in Cardiff needed enthusiastic journalistic endorsement. It was another of those significant steps on the road to creating something we can now identify as Welsh politics.

At the same time, though, it draws attention to one of the central questions raised by that journey. If people in Wales are to make more decisions for themselves, how are they to learn about what is at stake? Where is the journalism which is an essential component of an informed democracy? I'll look elsewhere at the role of broadcasting, but written journalism is an essential component of a pluralistic society. This is because newspapers are by their nature opinionated, prejudiced, erratic and, quite often, just plain wrong. That's why we need lots of them to provide a constituency of knowledge, opinion and debate. In this the merits or otherwise of *The Western Mail* at any given time are not relevant. This is an argument about quantity as much as quality.

In 1996 Thomson Regional Newspapers, the owners of *The Western Mail*, were taken over by Trinity Holdings, the owners of the *Daily Post* (formerly the *Liverpool Daily Post*) the only other morning newspaper which is aimed at a Welsh readership but which does not circulate in South Wales. Not only did this deal put those two papers into the same hands, it also meant that Trinity Holdings became the owners of the *South Wales Echo*, *Wales on Sunday* and the Celtic Press Group, which runs a large number of South Wales weekly papers.

The consequences of this pattern of ownership is not some kind of soviet-style editorial command (organisations like Trinity Holdings and its predecessors don't care what's in their papers as long as they make money) but a complete lack of any kind of independent newspaper constituency. There is no particular reason, for example, for *The Western Mail* to try again to build circulation in North Wales when it would do so at the expense of its sister paper, the *Daily Post*. At the same time there is little incentive for good journalists to remain in newspapers in Wales since there are few opportunities to advance themselves. Some do stay, of course, but the lack of a market is inevitably reflected in their pay and conditions. Freelance contributors soon discover that if they don't write for Trinity Holdings then they don't write.

From time to time people come to the conclusion that a

magazine or two might help plug this gap. These ventures are almost invariably doomed to failure, or at best a kind of life-in-death obscurity where contributors often seem to outnumber the readers, not least because it is impossible to sell enough copies to make them pay. One of the reasons they don't sell is because the shops won't stock them; the shops won't stock them because they don't sell. This is called economics. But it must be said, too, that these magazines are often rather unwelcoming to the average reader, grim even, with about as many laughs per thousand words as Arthur Scargill. Over the years they have come and gone – *Wales*, *Welsh Outlook* (two issues only in the nineteen-sixties) *The Anglo Welsh Review*, *Planet*, *Arcade*, the *New Welsh Review* and so on, but in most cases you might communicate just as efficiently by ringing up selected friends and reading them the text.

Yet it's virtually only in such magazines that any serious attempt is made at criticism of literature, theatre, music and, in particular, broadcasting which is elsewhere very often taken at the valuation of the institutions which provide it or as the source of gossip and free large photographs.

Book publishing, if anything, is even worse. There's no need to describe the merits or defects of the few who try to make some kind of business of it. The inescapable truth of the matter is that hardly anyone would bother writing a book to be published in Wales except out of vanity or a desire for some kind of professional advancement. Communication about common concerns through the written word is minimal. Argument about those concerns is almost non-existent.

What is particularly disturbing is that the condition I have described here, a shortage of journalism from within and without, is persisting at a time when people in Wales will have more influence over their own destinies than they've had, you can argue, since the thirteenth century. Worse, Welsh politics and the means of learning about it are actually going in opposite directions: the more we need to know about ourselves, the less information is provided. More than twenty years after the first devolution debate, Duncan Gardiner reflected on the way in which politics and the press in Wales might have an important inter-dependence. "What we were trying to prove was that

Wales did have its own identity and therefore needed its own national newspaper," he said.

In any generally accepted sense of the term 'national' it still doesn't have one and in any case it needs at least two or, better still, three, which is about as realistic an ambition as winning the National Lottery jackpot four weeks running. Even so, we can wonder or more accurately, dream, that the existence of a Welsh assembly might in some way provide the impetus towards mending an increasingly serious gap in the framework which sustains public life in Wales. After all, democracy isn't simply about voting a few more times, but about knowledge. Where, in these changed circumstances will Welsh people find it?

Perhaps the very existence of a new system will make Wales in itself more interesting to the outside world. Perhaps more of those who come to write will leave their little box of clichés at home. Perhaps Welsh writers will complain a little less often about how no-one in London loves them and just get on with it, seizing the rest of the world by the throat and making them listen. Perhaps, too, a media magnate of some kind, seeing that only thirteen per cent of people in Wales read Welsh-based newspapers, will think that there might just be another thirteen per cent willing to read another newspaper. Don't hold your breath.

Then again, people will perhaps argue that, at the end of the twentieth century, at the end of the millennium, we are talking about the wrong thing here, that the printed word is already in the process of being superseded. There are certain signs of it. When I worked on *The Western Mail* thirty years ago we saw the broadcasters as our rivals in news coverage as much as anything else. We assumed, not without some reason, that they wouldn't have any news at all if they didn't keep pinching ours. We would not mention their existence except when we were able to publish something to their detriment.

Nowadays in Wales and elsewhere it's generally accepted that television and radio are the prime sources of basic information – not least because as broadcasting has got faster newspapers have got slower. Printed journalism spends as much time on spin as it does on providing the raw material of fact. And in its turn what is happening in broadcasting, on screen and off screen, fills an increasing number of column inches. For such reasons, then perhaps we should be looking at television and radio to provide the independent journalism and robust criticism which are essential components of any democratic system, and in particular a new and delicate one such as that intended by a Welsh assembly.

As you might expect, it's nothing like as simple as that.

The Illusion Factory

If you slip around the back of the BBC's Welsh headquarters in Llantrisant Road, Llandaff, you'll eventually find yourself in High Street, a place that will seem familiar to most people who know Wales. There's a chip shop and, next to it, an ironmonger's. There's a cafe and a chemist's and a bank. It might be anywhere or nowhere and, in a sense, it's both, because this is High Street, Cwmderi, the home of the Welsh language soap opera *Pobol y Cwm*, a kind of tiny Welsh nod to the idea of the Hollywood studio lot. It's a place mainly of façades, appropriately enough, since it is a small section of one of those factories where, day after day, they manufacture the Welsh illusion. It's not the only one, but it's the biggest, BBC Wales being in effect the Microsoft Corporation of the Welsh image industry.

All broadcasting is like this. High Street, Cwmderi, is no different from Brookside or Albert Square or Coronation Street, in that it is the place in which is set an imagined, pre-fabricated, heightened, but recognisable version of a certain kind of life. And when I say *all* broadcasting I mean exactly that. It's a mistake to think it's just the drama departments that turn out a fictionalised account of our lives: everyone is making it up, in particular the people working in those two areas of production which present themselves to the public as the unflinching guardians of the truth – news and current affairs.

This is not to accuse of deception the hard-working and honest people who staff those departments in the BBC (in which I have worked myself for a large part of the last thirty years) or HTV or anywhere else for that matter. Journalists worry about getting things right rather more than the general public is inclined to allow them credit for, but the problem is that the very best any broadcaster can do is to give you a generalised approximation of what is going on in the world. The editorial process is a way of trying to impose some sort of order on chaos, and it is not for nothing that all items in news journalism are known as "stories".

This is particularly true in television news where the scarce raw material consists of pictures which, if you're very lucky, contain some element of drama on however tiny a scale. "Good pictures," people say encouragingly to each other, and then try to think of how to present them in a way that keeps the viewer at least within shouting distance of the truth. From time to time this is denounced as a reprehensible way of going on. The people who run broadcasting are particularly prey to cyclical change, or faddism as we call it, and their main motivation is not the restless search for innovation but a constant anxiety that they won't be doing what everyone else is doing. For a little while people go round talking about things like responsibility, duty to the public, the courage to be boring and all the rest of it, but soon enough the new philosophy falls into disrepute, a few people take early retirement and once again the cry of "good pictures" is heard throughout the land.

This is how it works. Some time in the seventies, when Jim Callaghan was Prime Minister, he was visiting a colliery in South Wales. In those days no colliery visit by a celebrity of any kind could be considered complete without the ritual presentation of a miniature miners' lamp. And no television report of the visit was judged authentic without pictures of that presentation. It was by no means exciting, but at least something moved in the frame.

On this particular occasion, though, there was a small disaster. As the lamp was being handed to the Prime Minister by a union official, there was one of those familiar moments when no-one was quite sure who was supposed to be holding the thing. It fell to the floor in a clatter of broken glass and buckled metal.

Back at base, intelligence of this stupendous event on a slow news day was received with tumultuous excitement. London was alerted. The world, thanks to the huge resources of BBC television and the vigilance of its reporters, even in places as remote as Cynheidre Colliery, Ammanford, would learn of the events of that day. As the BBC's Welsh Political Correspondent at that time I was the man on the case and, as I recall it now, the intention was to cut a piece of about fifty seconds which would contain the entire coverage of the Callaghan visit. The incident with the lamp would occupy perhaps fifteen or twenty seconds of this time.

Good pictures, we muttered to each other, but then a certain amount of unease crept in, certainly as far as I was concerned, although when a correspondent has doubts it's usually assumed he's trying to keep in with someone important. The problem was, though, that while the version of events we were planning would not exactly have been a lie, at the same time it would certainly not have been the truth. The incident had unmistakably happened, but we were nevertheless proposing to manufacture something dishonest out of it. The clear message would have been that the main event in the Prime Minister's day had been a momentary piece of clumsiness, and quite possibly not even his clumsiness. More important, it would have been, by implication, a comment on Callaghan's general competence and, by extension, that of his government, which some of my more combative colleagues thought made a particularly good reason for running it.

In the end, a most unusual event took place. Reason prevailed, as it does sometimes even in journalism, and the piece was never broadcast. On another day, with different editors, on the sort of day when people keep saying to each other, "Not much around", it probably would have been. And it's true that it would have been no more phoney than a great deal of other broadcasting, perhaps most of it. It was a reminder that the way in which life is deciphered for our television screens depends on an editorial process in which the vital elements are individual judgements on whatever fragments of raw material happen to come to hand. It's like trying to do a large jigsaw without the picture on the box.

Not that the Callaghan visit to Cynheidre went unreported. Eventually fifty seconds or so were transmitted on the network showing him relaxed and confident and talking briefly about some scheme or other which would make the world better for working people. His critics would have argued that that was dishonest too and they'd have had a case. But what we couldn't do, of course, was to show him going round all day not dropping miner's lamps before finally, in a dramatic denouement, just the one fell from his nerveless fingers. That might have been a bit nearer the truth, but it wouldn't have been television.

More than twenty years before the *Pobol y Cwm* set was built, at the time when I was the BBC's Welsh Industrial Correspondent, I suggested facetiously that we could save a lot of time and money by getting the BBC's designers to erect in the car park scenery representing the locations of our most regular news stories. Some pithead winding gear, perhaps, a factory gate to which we could summon members of Equity to take the part of pickets, a cardboard model of the outside of the Welsh Office and a hedge and farm gate to take care of any story set outside the industrial south.

All right, this wasn't funny because it wasn't funny, but it wasn't funny either because it was more or less true. The most famous pithead anywhere in Britain was at Nantgarw, near Pontypridd, not because it had any particular significance in the scheme of things, but because it was a few miles north of Cardiff and so the nearest colliery to any BBC newsroom. During the miners' strikes of 1972 and 1974 I lost count of the number of times I was asked to slip along to Nantgarw, stand in front of the winding gear and recite the details of the latest developments, or lack of them, in the dispute.

Wales was coal, even when Wales was ceasing to be coal, even, indeed, when it had ceased to be coal. At other times it would be druids or male voice choirs or Max Boyce or rugby players or any of those images that are both true and not true at one and the same time. Just as in written journalism, but even more so, broadcasters look for the familiar image which reassures them and their audience that the world is pretty much what they thought it was. In Wales, under the law of supply and demand as much as anything, we acquiesce in this process. We complain about the demand for clichés while at the same time handing them over the counter to our regular customers.

All of this wouldn't matter too much perhaps if it weren't for the fact that in Wales broadcasting is probably more important than it is anywhere else in the world. This is true in particular of cultural life, both in the creative, artistic meaning of the word, as well as in the sense of the commonly understood values and experiences we share. When it comes to drama, music, sport, religion, politics, the arts, news and all the rest of existence that isn't actually eating and sleeping, BBC Wales and HTV leave all other providers standing. Where else in the world apart from

BBC Wales, for example, could you send for your in-house symphony orchestra to record the signature tune for the nightly news programme? But there's much more to it than that because in the second, broader, cultural sense broadcasting might have been the most significant single influence in creating the place we now recognise as Wales.

In his book, *Broadcasting and the BBC in Wales*, the historian John Davies argues that "Wales could be defined as an artefact produced by broadcasting". His view is that the very idea of Wales as a unity was something that was created by the rise of broadcasting. He said in a later radio interview: "There was no such thing as all-Wales News until the coming of the BBC. The concept of Wales as a unity which had a news which could be announced daily was something which came into being with the BBC. You could argue that in a way the BBC created Wales. But that it was also the only significant all-Wales institution to come into existence between the nineteen-hundreds and the nineteen-fifties and sixties. The creation of the Welsh region of the BBC, as it was called in the mid-thirties, was a very profound and important event."

One of the revealing slogans of the reporting trade is that news is where journalists are, and the process this phrase describes meant that, particularly from the fifties onwards, there was an institutional response to the needs of broadcasters to fill their programmes.

"Once there is a platform from which to announce Welsh news, then there is almost a necessity to create Welsh news to fill that platform." In its turn, Davies says, that has altered within Wales people's attitudes to some of the central questions of identity. "There is a kind of momentum, a kind of logic in it that leads to the situation we have today where to talk of the news of Wales, to talk about Welsh devolution, government in Wales or the Welsh economy is no longer a laughable concept."

To some extent the influence of broadcasting was deliberately directed at creating this sense of Welsh unity. On a modest scale it could be the provider of many of the institutions, particularly cultural ones, which defined a nation and which Wales conspicuously lacked. In a lecture he gave in 1965, Hywel Davies, who was Head of Programmes for BBC Wales and who was to die young not long afterwards, defined this role when he said: "Broadcasting people should march, most of the time, in the vanguard of their society."

If they don't, who will? you might ask in Wales, and Geraint Stanley Jones, later a Controller of BBC Wales and then the BBC's first Managing Director of Regional Broadcasting, said he believed Hywel Davies's view encapsulated what the feeling and the expectation of those times actually was.

"He said, among other things, that broadcasting has to be the theatre, the concert hall, the debating chamber of life in Wales. There was an awareness that Wales was lacking in formal institutions in terms of things like music and theatre. We only had the university, the national library and the national Eisteddfod, but we had little else that you could call a national institution."

The two other institutions you could add to that list are, I suppose, the Welsh Rugby Union and the Football Association of Wales which also provide a national constituency of interest and, very often, despair, but the thrust of the argument remains. At the same time there's always a danger of over-stating this case, and while the broadcasters clearly had a significant effect on creating a Welsh context, particularly in politics, there were many times when they were marching hand-in-hand with other influences. For example, in February 1964 the Welsh Region of the BBC became BBC Wales, something which combined an expansion of the service with a new name that at least suggested a more independent existence. On October 15 of the same year Harold Wilson won the election (just) which led to the fulfilment of Labour's promise to create the post of Secretary of State for Wales with a seat in the Cabinet. The two events meant more Wales-wide events to broadcast about and a greater capacity to broadcast about them.

Broadcasting has been a crucial influence in the distinctive development of Welsh life, in particular in the story of the Welsh language. One can only look on in admiration and amazement at the seductive powers of those who managed to persuade not just a government, but a Conservative government headed by Mrs Thatcher at the height of her anti-handout zeal, to make millions of pounds of public money available to fund a

Welsh language television channel, and to make it available year after year. It was a brilliant trick and single-issue campaigners around the world must still wonder how it was done.

The clear message was that, in the everyday lives of ordinary people, by far the most important cultural influence was television. It seemed self-evident to many people that if television didn't consistently speak to people in their own language then that language, Welsh, was doomed. Not everyone subscribed to this point of view but it was an argument easily grasped, in particular by those people in government whose job it is to make this kind of decision. They can think of it as heritage and get a nice feeling of liberal-minded warmth as they hand over the dosh.

So far so good then, but is it possible that you can have too much of a good thing, even when it comes to saving the Welsh language? It's impossible to deny that S4C is a remarkable achievement. Providing the service it does on a population base of something like half a million is quite astonishing, a tribute to the talent, energy and determination of those who make the programmes and perform in them. The trouble is that, in a small world, it is also a sponge.

For example, for some years John Davies was warden of Pantycelyn Hall, a hostel for two hundred and fifty university students in Aberystwyth, and he became aware of the way in which broadcasting could almost overwhelm other aspects of Welsh language life.

"When you'd ask them what they wanted to do when they graduated, they'd smile coyly and say, 'Something in the media.' And these were people who a generation ago would have become teachers. Some of them would have been excellent teachers and there is nothing more important than awakening a pupil's mind at, say, thirteen to sixteen. That is the most important thing anyone can do in a lifetime. Compared to that, to make programmes is very small beer indeed, it seems to me. I do feel that people have been drawn from important things like teaching into the media and perhaps drawn from other things too – perhaps commercial life. The only thing we seemed to breed in Aberystwyth in the eighties were broadcasters and lawyers and I can't think of two less constructive elements in society."

Even so, what are people to do? Why should someone be expected to forsake a comfortable living, sometimes a very good one, as a producer or a reporter or a presenter in radio or television to work in an under-funded education system, or perhaps to write a novel in Welsh and be paid a handful of small change for doing so? It's not that people don't do these things, it's just that the resources of Welsh language life have to be spread very thinly to meet the needs of a pluralistic society and broadcasting makes perhaps disproportionate demands on them.

But broadcasting's influence is even wider, some people would argue more pernicious, than that because it is a significant industry as well as a cultural force. The BBC, HTV and S4C are all based in Cardiff and so make a magnet of that city and of South East Wales for anyone who wants to work for those organisations directly. Naturally enough many independent producers think that's the place to be too, because it creates the kind of network in which there is no real substitute for the rubbing of shoulders. Never underestimate the influence in any business of the easily-arranged lunch.

At the same time people have created a smaller branch of the industry in North West Wales in particular where production houses and facilities companies have flourished. However if S4C decides, as it did in 1997, that it doesn't want to commission as many programmes from those companies as it has in the past, then there are personal consequences for those who work for them and implications for the life of the communities in which they are based. So it is that S4C is important not only in how Welsh people see themselves but in how they work and live. And where they work and live come to that. In the end its influence might well be to reinforce further the metropolitan dominance of the South East where there might be Welsh signs above the veg in Tesco's but where the language of the streets is English.

This is the subject of some complaint, but S4C's job is to provide a television service, not to act as an instrument of cultural and social policy in the wider world. (That's what they say now, anyway, although it was not the line taken when Gwynfor Evans, its only begetter, was preparing to settle down in the study of his home in Llangadog and starve himself to

death if the Government refused to honour its promise to
establish it. It was culture, culture all the way then.) People
move on in their ideas and memories fade, but while people
salute the twin achievements of establishing the channel and of
making it work, in darker moments they sometimes ask if it
might not be, in the end, a disaster rather than a triumph for
the Welsh language.

This, though, isn't just about the Welsh language. In fact it's
not even mainly about the Welsh language, because what has
happened is that, perhaps inadvertently, the broadcasters have
invented a national agenda for English speakers in Wales. More
than that, they've created a nationalist agenda and if this seems
at first sight to be an exaggeration it's worth looking at, as a
small example, the jingoistic style in which rugby internationals
are regularly promoted on television. The fact that Wales almost
invariably lose only serves to feed further the sense of wounded
national pride and the general all-round unfairness of life as
currently organised.

For a long time the passions that broadcasting issues aroused
in Welsh political argument were less to do with empowering
Welsh speakers as freeing those who spoke only English. It is
perhaps largely forgotten now that the agreement to create S4C
met with general approval in Wales not because it would sustain
a particular culture, but because it would get rid of it. Get rid
of it, that is, from the sight of the average Welsh television
viewer who wanted English language programmes on all channels
uninterrupted by output he found entirely incomprehensible. It
is in any case almost impossible to over-estimate the vehemence
of the average viewer's insistence that he or she should have
available at all times the same television as everyone else in the
United Kingdom. Television schedulers will tell you of the
streams of abusive phone calls that used to follow an occasional
decision to move – *move*, not cancel – an episode of that particularly dreadful late-night Australian, lesbian, prison soap opera,
Cell Block H.

The final disposition was a solution that provided for a sense
of unity, and once S4C was under way in 1982, protecting the
couch potato majority from any Welsh language programmes,
there was now more room for an English language agenda on

television and a less irritated audience to receive it. It was also another important step in the enlargement of a particular class of broadcaster in Wales – those who spoke only English.

In both BBC Wales and HTV there had long been a premium on bilingualism. In areas like news, for example, the same people would be called upon to produce programmes and bulletins in both languages and so it was a practical necessity. It was not an invariable rule, but for many years after I joined the staff of BBC Wales in 1970, I was the object of some curiosity, especially among those working in other parts of the BBC outside Wales. "You don't speak Welsh, so how did you get the job?" they'd ask in tones which implied at the very least the existence of some powerful Masonic uncle. As it happened, my predecessor hadn't been a Welsh speaker either, but there was scarcely a senior job in the whole organisation for which the advertisement didn't carry the familiar rubric: Welsh essential.

This condition was eroded by the expansion of broadcasting which has brought us to the present position where BBC Wales has divided its Welsh and English language broadcasting services, and where HTV's output for its own channel is entirely in English, although it remains, on a commercial basis, a producer of Welsh language programmes for S4C. The extent of the broadcasting explosion can be judged from the fact that BBC Wales now provides four separate news services – two in each language – for television and radio.

But perhaps the most significant event took place some time before the changes involved in the creation of a Welsh language television channel. This was the arrival, in November 1978, of Radio Wales. It has been forcibly argued that the establishment of Radio Wales was the single most important happening in the history of Welsh broadcasting, and by extension, therefore, it was an event of enormous weight in the history of Welsh politics. It was the institutionalisation of the idea of a separate, English-speaking Wales.

As BBC Wales's Head of Programmes at the time, Geraint Stanley Jones was responsible for its creation as a distinct service, complete in itself, instead of being an opt-out of the UK network. "The concept of Radio Wales is that you have a listener who listens only to Radio Wales, that he lives his life through the concept of what is produced on Radio Wales. Now, given the nearness of Wales to England and the nearness in terms of airwaves, that is not a reality, but the way it is scheduled and produced one would think that Radio Wales was a nation." In other words, even if, as Jones says, all broadcasting is an illusion, if Radio Wales exists, then Wales must exist too. One of the most teasing questions about this is whether this English-speaking Wales, with its overlapping but not identical concerns with Welsh-speaking Wales, would ever have been created without the existence of the Welsh language and the special care that has been lavished upon it. It's no good pretending that there has not been persistent resentment at the apparently privileged treatment handed out to the language, particularly, if not exclusively, among those who think it's denied them jobs. What about "our boys"? was how it was once put to me by a monoglot trade unionist as he surveyed the BBC, an expression of envy and of that imperative of human nature which says that if something's being handed out, we've got to have some of it too. Even so, in the creation of a larger Welsh world for those who speak only English, John Davies believes the existence of the two languages side by side is a crucial one.

"I very much doubt if the structure that we've had would have come into existence without the motto that was represented by the aspirations of those who were concerned with the Welsh language. English language programmes have grown side by side with them and I doubt if you'd have had Radio Wales had there not been an impetus to have Radio Cymru."

It's quite probable that without the influence of broadcasting there would have been no Welsh assembly, but in its turn the creation of that body will increase the importance of broadcasting, particularly in the light of the meagre provision, as I've said, of other Welsh journalism. The problem is, though, that as the nature of government in Britain, and in Wales in particular, heads in one direction, that of broadcasting is heading in another. Devolution and centralisation are passing each other on opposite carriageways of the M4.

There are many words and phrases to be wary of in the English language, ways of saying one thing while meaning the opposite. So it's always with a sense of foreboding that I hear

some BBC executive or other express the corporation's continued commitment to the regions. That usually means that the
corporation has rediscovered Manchester, as it does every five
years or so, and there is a great flurry of excitement as less
favoured departments are sent to re-establish themselves there.
More than that, I've found it a useful rule in life to beware of
anyone reaffirming his commitment to anything, since it is usually
a prelude to a complete change of course. John Major, for
example, would regularly declare his total confidence in some
beleaguered minister shortly before accepting his resignation.

For a long time "Head of Regions" was treated as a joke title
in the BBC, one that was taken out and dusted down whenever
some senior executive was found to be incompetent in some
way or, more frequently, fell out of favour with people even
more senior than him. Announcements would be made contain-
ing reassuring words about the delicate and crucial nature of the
task the victim was being asked to perform and that was pretty
well the end of him, apart from the retirement party a couple of
years later.

But no longer. In 1987 the BBC decided to create a serious
organisation called the Directorate of Regional Broadcasting.
Geraint Stanley Jones was its first managing director and, as
such, at the highest levels of BBC management. When it all
began, he says, the intention, or the sales pitch, was that it
would strengthen the regions, in particular what the BBC calls,
in a typical piece of political tightrope-walking, the national
regions – Wales, Scotland and Northern Ireland – which are
thus nations and regions at one and the same time.

"There was a general feeling that broadcasting in the national
regions in terms of representation was only a matter of grace
and favour. If you had a sympathetic director-general then you
had the ear of somebody, but there was no structure that gave
you a place on the board of management. So this directorate was
created in London in order to give a voice, to push devolution
downwards."

For a time, Jones says, it worked, but the BBC is a big business and the natural inclinations of big business reasserted
themselves. "There's always this tendency to revert to the
centre, particularly at times of political and financial stress. The

easy answer always in a large institution like the BBC is to say that we want to cut back and we're worried about value for money and all those things and we've got to have tighter control at the centre."

We have to remember that there never was a golden age when the BBC regions got on with whatever they were doing largely free of interference from the centre. There was a brief period in the late seventies and early eighties, Geraint Stanley Jones recalls, when BBC Wales was as autonomous as it had ever been, but not for long. "It's gone back again because at the end of the day I have had to recognise that all of us who didn't work in London were fighting against the concept that it was a branch line. It really is BBC London."

This isn't something about which people should be surprised in the context of the pressures of modern television. Because it's funded by two billion pounds in licence fees, the BBC is constantly under pressure to justify its existence, particularly in the size of the audiences it gets, a condition which increases the emphasis on network production and delivering that uniform product throughout the country which the viewers demonstrably crave.

In this the BBC is in competition most directly at present with ITV, where Mrs Thatcher's Government made changes which inevitably meant the end of the specifically regional character with which the system was established. (It's interesting, by the way, that despite the devolutionary pressures of recent years the ITV franchise has continued to embrace both Wales and the West of England, so that the two parts of the company continue to go round together like Siamese twins with very different interests.)

The system of blind bidding for franchises introduced by the Broadcasting Act of 1990 meant in the end that the ITV companies would have less money to spend on the actual business of broadcasting. The consequence of that was a greater need to maximise revenue to pay the costs of those blind bids. Serious money in ITV comes from network broadcasting, so the result is further pressure on regional programmes. The independent regional companies have largely disappeared into the Grimpen Mire of the media conglomerates, a process which has claimed HTV among many others.

It's probable that the substance of these changes was in any case inevitable as the character of broadcasting was revolutionised. Satellite, cable and digital systems mean there is simply going to be a vast amount more of it and the influence on our view of the world of the huge corporations, publicly owned or commercial but regulated, will be much diminished. They themselves recognise it clearly enough, and the BBC and ITV companies are devoting an increasing amount of their time to finding other ways of retaining the privileges of a charter and a licence fee, or of continuing to make money as best they can.

While this process may be looked on largely with indifference elsewhere, it once again raises a pressing question in Wales. How can we know about ourselves and our condition at a time when we are expected to take more responsibility for that condition? Of course broadcasters will go on broadcasting about Wales, the news will tell us who said what, current affairs programmes will name the guilty men, sports commentators will explain how a new coach is about to transform the fortunes of the Welsh rugby XV, and life and how and what we learn of it will carry on very much as it always has. Well, that's not quite true, actually because, whatever the changes in the system, BBC Wales and HTV Wales remain public service broadcasters and therefore will give us even more as they cover the work of the Welsh Assembly with vigilance etc.

This contribution is not to be underestimated, although it by no means fills the gap left by the lack of diversity in Welsh printed journalism, and at least two issues will be raised which will perhaps threaten to reduce it further. The first is a proposal that is made from time to time that, following the successful example of S4C, an English language television service should be established carrying the products of BBC Wales and HTV Wales which are now transmitted on their respective networks. This is an idea which is both innocent and menacing at one and the same time.

It's innocent because it blithely ignores the commercial interests involved in HTV, for example, but it's menacing because it would mean even less nourishment for the emaciated pluralism that exists at the moment. You could well find, for example, that the BBC would become the sole source of broadcast news

– a kind of Welsh Ministry of Truth. Then again, a single television employer would mean twice as much prospect of being permanently unemployed if you failed to please the right person. The people who put forward this sort of scheme talk a lot about democracy but they don't know what it means.

Even so, this proposal is bound to be raised again, and probably even more pressingly. That's because the other cloud on the horizon is that of broadcasting itself becoming part of the political agenda. In setting up the Welsh assembly the Labour Government recognised this clearly enough and left authority in this area with the Department of Culture, Media and Sport, itself an ominously Orwellian title. But why shouldn't the assembly take responsibility, particularly when you consider how important broadcasting is in Wales as a method of communication, as an influence on events and as an employer?

To take a simple example, why is it that the UK Culture Secretary should appoint the Chairman of S4C? When I asked him that question I was told that, naturally, the appointment was made in the closest consultation with the Welsh Office. In that case why shouldn't Welsh Office take complete responsibility now to be followed, in the fullness of time, by the decision being made by the assembly as part of the process in which flames will start licking round the promised bonfire of the quangos?

The answer isn't simply that the bonfire might actually turn out to be little more than a Kozeeglo flame-effect room heater, rather than a decent blaze, but also that the assembly would be tempted to interfere as much as it could in broadcasting matters, to debate annually, for instance, the state of the industry and its performance within the governance of Wales. It particular it won't escape the notice of members looking for things to do that S4C is now funded directly from taxation, that more than seventy million pounds a year goes directly from the Treasury to sustain it. It might not be much to the chaps in Whitehall, but it would be a huge sum to those sitting in Cardiff Bay, especially as they would find most of the expenditure for which they were nominally responsible already spoken for. Human nature being what it is, and Wales being what it is, they might be tempted to shave a bit off that broadcasting budget ("Shall we say ten per cent?") to meet the pressures of social priorities which are, and will continue to be, many. We can all write the speeches now: "Of course the language is very important, Mr Chairman, but as long as our schools decay and waiting lists grow longer in our hospitals...." Fill in the blanks with pressing social needs.

As things stand the assembly is not allowed into the playground, but we are talking here about politicians and, as night follows day, they'll soon want to know why not. That is what politicians do, that is what defines politicians and, the broadcasters who have been instrumental in creating a new way of political life may now find their own lives changed by it. As long ago as 1945 the Labour Party was putting forward schemes for a Welsh Broadcasting Corporation. That could well return to a higher position on the political agenda with a much better prospect of it being an ambition fulfilled.

It's all the more likely because of the curious way in which the assembly has been created and its powers awarded or withheld. It's all rather reminiscent of the master work of Baron Frankenstein who assembled spare body parts as best he could and then harnessed a thunderstorm (the referendum?) to put some life into the creature. In the end he proved rather less tractable than Frankenstein had hoped and, you will recall, got particularly cross with his master when he failed to provide a girl monster. In much the same way, who can say for certain now that a frustrated assembly won't break out and carry off a few virgins for company, among whom the broadcasters might well find themselves numbered.

The Day Before Yesterday

The problem was, the teacher explained, that the Welsh Joint Education Committee insisted on all candidates sitting its 'O' level history examination answering at least one question about Wales. The good thing was, he went on, that the WJEC also appreciated the fact that there wasn't all that much Welsh history about. Therefore the examiners always included some question about the Acts of Union which constitutionally joined Wales and England in 1536 and 1543. He would provide us with the necessary information on the subject and that, as far as we were concerned, would be as much as any adolescent would need to know about his or her own past.

That little scene took place in the late fifties, and no doubt happened all over Wales. But not much more than a quarter of a century later anyone with a television set anywhere in Britain could scarcely escape the fact that there was, after all, much more to it than that. In 1984, once a week for six weeks, viewers to BBC 2 (and BBC Wales) were exposed to the full force of Dai Smith's fierce analysis of Welsh historical themes. Over on HTV Wales (and Channel 4) Gwyn A. Williams, another professional historian whose passion, like Smith's, was in inverse proportion to his size, slugged it out with the broadcaster Wynford Vaughan Thomas for thirteen weeks as they romped and quarrelled their way through the story of Wales from the prehistoric to the post-industrial. Alongside these three guys the Ancient Mariner was tongue-tied and reticent.

Gwyn (or Gwyn Alf as he became widely known in his last years) was particularly influential in the progress Welsh history made so rapidly from a subject briefly acknowledged in the grammar school classroom to its central place in the understanding of what Wales now is and how it got there. He was brilliant in conversation, compelling as a lecturer, magnetic if dangerous company, uncompromising as a writer, tiny, handsome, seductive, vain, quick to take offence, neurotic, funny, furious and, quite often, totally impossible. He created both disciples and detractors and his famous stammer, which racked

149

his body and which could impart an almost unbearable dramatic tension to his public and private performances, was widely imitated in both the academic and broadcasting worlds.

Gwyn's significance, though, doesn't lie simply in his personal flamboyance and in what he wrote and broadcast, but at least as much in his setting the pace for younger Welsh historians, in particular the post-war generation twenty years his junior, who were to reinvestigate our past and explain how it informed our present lives.

There were less overtly exotic influences. David Williams, for example, Professor of Welsh History at Aberystwyth, was born in 1900 and was apparently the embodiment of cautious, Welsh, Nonconformist respectability, meticulous and exacting in his historian's trade. He was all that, but also a waspish, oblique commentator on the follies of fellow academics and students, about which he knew far more than a stranger might ever have suspected. When he published his brilliant one-volume survey, *A History of Modern Wales*, in 1950, he was laying foundations on virgin territory. And his work on Chartism and on the Rebecca Riots marked a shift towards the social history which was to become the central area of study for so many of the people he taught.

Twenty years younger than David, Glanmor (later Sir Glanmor) Williams introduced a change of emphasis in Swansea where he became Professor of History in Swansea in 1957. Peter Stead went there in 1961 and remained in the department, as a student and later a lecturer, for more than thirty-five years.

"Glanmor Williams was a very, very remarkable man. He was a Tudor historian but, I think uniquely in the early nineteen-sixties, saw the way things were going. He told his colleagues in the very small history department that they could go on teaching medieval and early modern history but that above all they were going to have to teach modern history. He said, too, that we should be committed to the social history of modern Wales. He made that decision and it was a revolutionary decision."

In 1960 Glanmor Williams founded *The Welsh History Review*, which has a continuing influence, and many of the people who were to make substantial reputations as historians –

Kenneth O. Morgan, Dai Smith, John Davies, Hywel Francis are included among them – spent at least a part of their careers at Swansea. But this was not some kind of spontaneous Welsh phenomenon. Throughout Britain historians, left-wing historians in particular, were turning away from the traditional emphasis put on crown and parliament as the backbone of the study of the subject and concentrating instead on the lives of the millions rather than of the few. It was a change that gripped many at that time, including Dai Smith.

"Suddenly people were saying, 'Look, important history isn't constitutional history, it isn't the history of kings and queens, it isn't diplomatic history, it's about the history of ordinary people. It's labour history, it's cultural history.'

"I think in the nineteen-sixties for Wales history became an important, a defining issue, because it was only then that people were sufficiently removed from those searing experiences of the twenties and thirties and, of course, the War. It was only with my post-war generation that you had a group for whom the 1914-18 War and the 1926 General Strike were in a sense as distant, as intriguing and could be as objectively assessed as, let's say, 1831 or the Wars of the Roses."

When I went to Aberystwyth as a student in 1959 there was scarcely a textbook to be found on the subject of Welsh history. J.E. Lloyd's two-volume work took us to the Edwardian Conquest and 1282; David Williams's *Modern Wales* went from 1485 to 1939 in fewer than three hundred pages. We were urged, in the absence of other texts, to get hold of copies of *Wales Through the Ages*, the printed version of a series of talks commissioned by A.J. Roderick of the BBC's Welsh schools department, an astonishing project, unthinkable now, which brought together a stupendous collection of academics. The first lecture, *The First People*, was by the Cambridge archaeologist and early telly don, Glyn Daniel; the last, *The Rise of the House of Tudor*, was by David Williams.

The following year a second volume, no less ambitious, took the story from *The Threshold of the Modern Age*, by Glyn Roberts, to *The Rise of Labour*, by T.I. Jeffreys-Jones, the Warden of Coleg Harlech. At that stage Gwyn A. Williams was still officially a medievalist, but his talk, *The Emergence of a*

Working-Class Movement, was an indication of what was to come. Peter Stead, then a schoolboy, heard it.

"I remember sitting by the radio and listening to Gwyn Alf Williams talking about the Merthyr Riots and about Dic Penderyn being the first martyr of the Welsh working class and the impact of that was electrifying. It was partly his voice. We'd never heard a scholar, a historian, talking with that kind of Valleys accent and his stutter which added tremendous dramatic effect. Suddenly, this was our history. It was a real coming home and I would say I became a Welsh labour historian on the evening of that broadcast."

Once you looked at history from this perspective then Wales became, not a historical desert in which the occasional oasis was fringed with a few palm trees marked "Owain Glyndŵr" or "Acts of Union", but a fertile land virtually overgrown with the story of Welsh people. "When you think of the Welsh industrial civilisation of the nineteenth century," Peter Stead said, "how many people could you name? How many miners or steelworkers could you name? Of course we could name a few. We could name our grandfathers and in some cases our parents and we started with that. We started writing from our own experience and we were rescuing people from anonymity."

Some work had already begun before the young men of the sixties began to explore the possibilities of social history. Robin Page Arnot, for instance, had already been working for decades on the history of the Miners' Federation of Great Britain. He was asked to tackle the history of the South Wales miners as well. By 1975 he had published two volumes about Wales, taking the story as far as 1926. He was in a race with time he wasn't going to win.

It was during that period that, when the NUM's annual conference was held in Llandudno, Page Arnot was presented with an award to mark his work so far. A very old man, wearing a round, velvet smoking cap, he replied to the honour with a speech of surprising vigour. But as he left the rostrum the miners' President, Joe Gormley, admonished him cheerfully, and with characteristic tact: "Now, don't you go dying before you've finished writing that book." He did, of course.

By now a new sense of urgency had entered the field. In

1970, *Llafur*, the society for the study of Welsh labour history, had been founded, bringing together academics and the people, miners in particular but others too, whose history they were writing. Two of those closely involved, Hywel Francis and Dai Smith, together wrote *The Fed* which, in 1980, in a single volume, at last took the account of the South Wales Miners into recent times.

None of this is to say that a renewed interest in history, and an interest in a new kind of history, suddenly seized the Welsh nation. There weren't queues outside the bookshops eager for the latest news of, say, the Merthyr Rising of 1831, but this energy and productivity informed and partly created national debate. And coming largely from the left it inevitably brought resonances to the industrial turmoil which particularly characterised the politics of the nineteen-seventies. The two big miners' strikes of that period were themselves the material of history and part of its continuity. Just as important, perhaps more so, history was also, as Dai Smith says, part of the immediate political process. "There was still a sense in which you could alter contemporary political activity. However idealistic and ultimately utopian this might seem now, that's what it felt like then."

It was inevitable that this kind of conviction should knock on the door of a wider consciousness, and that it should do so in particular through the media. Not least because historians could make up for the institutional failings of journalism in Wales which I have already described and which persist. Here were people with something to say and highly-developed abilities in the art of saying it, who had already done much of the hard work in the archives and who could now be interpreted to a wider public. Television producers smile contentedly in their sleep when they dream of such characters. But it was perhaps a mixture of coincidence and clairvoyance which led us in the early eighties, both BBC Wales and HTV, to take up our history at the very time when, as we were to discover almost simultaneously, it was in the process of being dislocated. The past we were describing in 1984 was accessible and recognisable then in a way it would not be only a decade later.

The illumination this process provides can be seen in one of the documentaries I made after I had been recruited by the indefatigable Selwyn Roderick to the small team making that enigmatically punctuated series *Wales! Wales?* for the BBC. Our task, essentially, was to interpret Dai Smith's work for television, something which I have to say had both intellectually and temperamentally testing aspects to it. But so it was that in February 1983 I found myself in the Rhondda looking for the answer to one of the most nagging questions of twentieth-century Welsh history: did Winston Churchill send troops into Tonypandy in 1910 to confront striking miners?

In fact the question itself, and in particular its persistence, is at least as interesting as the answer. For my money much of the evidence is unambiguous: Churchill did give permission for the troops to move in and there are contemporary photographs available of Hussars riding through the streets of Llwynypia. But did the troops actually fire on the crowds? At the time Churchill told the King and Parliament that they had not done so. It wasn't a story believed in South Wales, though, and even in 1950 he was moved to repeat his denials at a political meeting at Ninian Park in Cardiff. But if, as he always insisted, the only contact with the rioters had been by the Metropolitan Police armed with rolled-up mackintoshes how had one miner, Samuel Rays, been killed?

This argument is now so familiar that it's virtually a tourist attraction. It still breaks out from time to time between academics or politicians. And in many ways it's the argument itself that's important, the way in which it captures so vividly the tensions between workers and owners, workers and government, the shift from Liberal Wales to Labour Wales, and so illuminates a whole social and economic order. In this story Churchill represents one set of values and attitudes, Tonypandy another. It's a kind of allegory and in this way a close-up account brings you the feel of a place and a time as well as the narrative of events. The idea was, as Dai Smith says, to use the techniques of the novelist as well as that of the historian.

As it happened, we had to interrupt the filming of this story in the summer of 1983 as some of us were diverted to coverage of the general election which was to see Mrs Thatcher re-elected with a majority of 144. That majority was to underpin her resolve to face down the national miners' strike, led by Arthur

Scargill, which began the next year and went on into 1985. In its turn that strike owed much of its character – on both sides – to history; and not just comparatively recent events, like 1972 or 1974, but the more distant past which particularly informs attitudes in those industries, like mining, which are built on exclusive communities. To know about Tonypandy in 1910 was to understand better what happened and what people felt as miners clashed with police at Orgreave in 1984.

The story of Tonypandy also illustrates another important role history has to play in contemporary life. That is that what people have believed about those events has been just as important as what actually did or didn't take place. That's why in the cinemas of South Wales audiences would jeer at Churchill as newsreels showed him going about his Prime Ministerial business in the nineteen-fifties. The inheritors of the people of Tonypandy in 1910 were sitting in the one-and-nines and it still mattered to them.

In the last film in the *Wales! Wales?* series we specifically looked at the persistence of the idea of Wales despite the events of centuries which had apparently threatened to overwhelm it. And in making this film we came across another example of the way in which the image can take on a life of its own. This was the case of the Welsh Not, the badge of shame famously hung around the necks of defiant or unlucky schoolchildren in the late nineteenth and early twentieth centuries when they persisted in speaking Welsh.

This has a significant place in the nationalist version of history in particular and both Dai and I were under the impression, encouraged by various television dramas, that this instrument was about the size of a small plank secured to the linguistically delinquent child by a piece of rope approximately the thickness of a ship's cable. When we went to the Welsh Folk Museum (now the Museum of Welsh Life) at St Fagans to see an example, however, it turned out to measure about two inches by one, with the initials 'W.N.' cut into it. It was not that it didn't exist, or that people weren't right to question its use, but as the distance between us and it grew with the years, so it came to fill an increasingly large part in the imagination and in folk history. For some people it had become the linguistic equivalent of the scarlet letter – 'A' for adultery – imposed on Wales by an alien authority, even if it was nothing of the kind.

But this is another example of the fact that understanding the present by interpreting the past is by no means a literal matter. Even if historians can agree on facts which, as is evident from the case of Tonypandy, isn't as easy as you might think, Marxists will then give you one interpretation, nationalists another, conservatives a third and so on. History is a debate, not a football match in which one side is declared the winner at the end of ninety minutes, or even after a penalty shoot-out. So, for example, in 1962 and 1973, Michael Foot produced the two volumes of his biography of Aneurin Bevan from which Bevan emerges as a pretty well unflawed political giant.

Then, in 1987, John Campbell produced what was described as the Social Democrat version of the life, *Nye Bevan and the Mirage of British Socialism*. The title alone tells you most of what you need to know about Campbell's view of Bevan's political philosophy. The consequence of that was Michael Foot constantly urging Dai Smith, and urging other people to urge Dai Smith, to write another book in refutation of Campbell's view.

As it happened it didn't work out quite like that, and although he was to write further about Bevan, Dai continued the debate in another form, in a documentary we made for BBC 2 in 1988. It was a specific attempt to throw light on the condition of the Labour Party at that time by looking at Bevan's career and ideas – in particular because of Bevan's continuing influence on one of the main protagonists but also because, in a wider sense, Bevan was long used as a touchstone of political rectitude in the Labour Party. It's all the more curious, actually, that his career is often summoned in support of some Conservative attack on Labour even though there was no man more reviled by the Tories of his day, a sentiment he returned with interest.

"Well, here we had, didn't we," Dai Smith said, "Neil Kinnock who was Leader of the Labour Party? Michael Foot had been so before him and Jim Callaghan before that. Three Welsh MPs, or three MPs representing three Welsh constituencies, and in Kinnock's case actually coming from Bevan's home town. There were these terrible civil wars raging within the

Labour Party. You remember at that time Bevan was continually cited by Neil Kinnock from platform after platform as a kind of guiding light. So that film was a serious attempt to say: what is it that Bevan teaches? What is it that Bevan shows us now? How would Bevan have responded? I still think that's a good quest."

Bevan's story was particularly apt at that time because Labour was already launched on its journey to the future that was to be Tony Blair, and even then the direction in which it was travelling was becoming clear. At the party conference in Bournemouth three years previously, Kinnock had publicly denounced the extreme Left as represented by the Militant activists in Liverpool, but thirty years before that it was Bevan, his hero, who was vilified by some, first as a Left-wing wrecker, but later as a betrayer of the Left. In the Labour Party of 1988, unilateral nuclear disarmament remained at the centre of the argument. In 1957 Bevan, back in the leadership of the party, had shattered his friends with the scorn he poured on the idea. Even forty years on, to hear those withering words: "You call that statesmanship? I call it an emotional spasm," is to experience a great jolt, like a shot suddenly ringing out in the theatre.

But just as shocking, in a different way, was Kinnock's Bournemouth speech. Even if its content could have been more easily predicted than that of Bevan's onslaught, its tone was electrifying, in particular because for many years the Left had counted Kinnock as one of their own. When Labour lost the 1959 General Election, people began to suggest that the party could never hold office again. The Conservatives had a majority of a hundred and commentators started to talk, as they often do, of a realignment of radical elements and specifically about a Lib-Lab pact. It was in those circumstances, less than a year before he died, that Bevan as Deputy Leader made a conference speech which was aimed particularly at binding up the party's wounds and which, was a restatement of his central belief in parliamentary democracy (something he preached as a revolutionary creed, Michael Foot argued) and consequently his vehement opposition to Communism. Change that word to Trotskyism and you have a straight line to the Kinnock speech a quarter of a century later.

"I am a social democrat," Bevan said. "I believe that it is possible for a modern intelligent community to organise its economic life rationally, with decent orders of priority, and it is not necessary to resort to dictatorship in order to do it."

As late as 1988 Labour was still a party greatly influenced by its past, trapped by it, some people came to argue, and so a great figure like Bevan could not be ignored but had to be explained in the modern context. Sometimes it had an almost theological aspect as people like Barbara Castle and Michael Foot told you what Bevan meant by what he said or, perhaps, how he might simply have got carried away by his own command of language and the reaction of his audience and so said things he didn't mean at all. The participants have been greatly helped in this process of interpretation by the fact that Bevan wrote little in which he revealed (or explained) himself.

It is in this way that the political debate in Wales came to be conducted by historians rather than journalists, in particular because they could to some extent offer the pluralism that, as I have already argued, is so clearly lacking in the day-to-day accounts of our affairs provided by newspapers and broadcasting. Very little in the past is so incontrovertible that it isn't susceptible to different interpretation by a nationalist historian, or a Marxist historian or a social democratic historian or, as John Davies argues, a combination of those things.

"A Marxist, nationalist historian with social democratic leanings which some of us are trying to be. We can claim to be a little bit genuine and are trying within our lights to bring forward an argument that is intelligible and that is founded on the available facts. I mean, almost everybody who writes is coloured by his background, his views, but I think the effort to be a little bit genuine is perhaps stronger than some people would be ready to admit."

One reason for that is perhaps that professional historians, whose work has to withstand the scrutiny of other professionals, are, in theory at least, rather more scrupulous than those who use history as a weapon in their social and political battles. The fact is, though, that the dividing line between the academic and the journalistic has become increasingly blurred. I used to think that the phrase 'contemporary history' was oxymoronically meaningless when I first heard it, perhaps in the mid-seventies, but it has come to describe the real world of study. In March 1991, Kenneth Clarke, who was then Secretary of State for Education, laid it down that for the purposes of the National Curriculum history was what took place up to twenty years previously. After that it was current affairs or, to use the official Government term, lies. Now, though, with deference and discretion largely absent from public life, the period over which events become history can be taken as the length of time it takes to write and publish a volume of memoirs.

The question that now arises is whether this process in which people have been offered a coherent description of Wales through its past will continue, or whether it will turn out to be only a short-lived flowering of interest and creativity. The world in which this exploration took place and which supported it has already changed, if not quite beyond recognition, at least in very significant ways.

It's clear, for example, that the academic world has become much less congenial for many people. Gwyn Alf was one of those who leapt, quite late in his career admittedly, into full-time television, threatening his audience in a succession of documentaries that if they didn't bloody well listen then he'd jump through the screen and stamp on their heads until they did. Others, like Peter Stead, who also abandoned his university early, have been drawn to what's called popular culture, a line of study which non-academics believe is little more than an excuse to watch television and read detective stories all day. Stead, as you might expect, explains it somewhat differently.

"Popular culture is a very, very important part of the history of Wales and of the UK generally. If you look at the history of sport, the history of acting, the history of music, you begin to see that what's important in Welsh history is the way in which energies have been released.

"We were historians of Welsh urban culture. Those of us who came out of the Wales of the immediate post-war period, although we were historians our real heroes were the rugby players of that era and the actors of that era, perhaps Richard Burton in particular, and we saw them as the best adverts for our culture."

This is perhaps another step in our changed attitude to history and to our understanding of our own world now. Having looked behind the kings and queens, the statesmen, the diplomats and the generals, and discovered the people, there is a greater compulsion to examine the way in which they have expressed their lives, in particular through those activities like sport and film and television, which have encapsulated their experience and aspirations.

For this reason it's less surprising that someone like Dai Smith who, after all, was the co-author of a book on Welsh rugby, should have left the world of the professional historian and his professorial chair, to preside over probably the single most important expression of popular culture in contemporary Wales – English language programming at BBC Wales. It's only a couple of miles by road, but surely it's a long way emotionally and intellectually. On the contrary, Dai says, it's simply the same ride on a different bus.

"Those of us who have lived in Wales and wished to talk and write and think and be about Wales will find various ways to articulate that sense of Welshness. I think you can be a historian one day, a novelist the next, a poet, a broadcaster. There are so few of us you've all got to go round the board. Maybe we've got to keep moving. You know, like that boy in the school photograph who goes from one end to the other and appears twice."

Which is, of course, another illusion, something in keeping with the world which between us – newspapermen, broadcasters and historians in particular – we have tried in different ways to illuminate. All three are imperfect trades in which the truth remains an elusive commodity, and our versions of it are often shaped by chance, experience and character. Between us we have tried to describe what the country is and in the process we have inevitably contributed to what is has become. You can't avoid the force of the accusation that we've invented Wales but, just as important, we've discovered it as well.

Index

About the Author

Patrick Hannan is a writer, broadcaster and journalist. During his career he has been Industrial Editor of *The Western Mail* and for thirteen years he was the BBC's Welsh Political Correspondent. As a television producer he has made documentaries for BBC2, BBC Wales and HTV. For many years he has been a regular writer and presenter for Radio 4. He has been a newspaper columnist and has contributed to a wide variety of publications as well as being the editor of two books on broadcasting in Wales. He presents a daily current affairs programme on Radio Wales as well as other programmes.